Alpha Beta

Alpha Beta

TED WHITEHEAD

FABER AND FABER
London . Boston

First published in 1972
by Faber and Faber Limited
3 Queen Square London WC1
Reprinted 1981
Printed in Great Britain by
Whitstable Litho Ltd., Whitstable, Kent
All rights reserved

ISBN 0 571 09974 2

All enquiries regarding amateur or professional production of this play should be addressed in the first instance to Margaret Ramsey Ltd., 14a Goodwin's Court, St. Martin's Lane, London WC2.

© *1972 by E. A. Whitehead*

for Kathleen and Kate and Helen

The action of the play occurs in the lounge of the Elliots' home in Liverpool, over a period of nine years. When the play opens Mr. Elliot is 29 and Mrs. Elliot 26.

ACT I: 1000 WOMEN—Winter, 1962

ACT II: PSEUDOMORPH—Spring, 1966

ACT III: ALPHA BETA—Summer, 1971

Alpha Beta opened at the Royal Court Theatre on 26th January 1972 and subsequently transferred to the Apollo Theatre. Albert Finney played Mr. Elliot and Rachel Roberts Mrs. Elliot. The play was directed by Anthony Page, designed by Alan Tagg and presented by the Royal Court Theatre and Memorial Enterprises.

Production Note

Alpha Beta is partly a study of moral conditioning but also explores the problem of a relationship in which, for complex reasons, one party is immeasurably more committed than the other. In production, these levels can be suggested by maintaining a minute naturalism on the surface but allowing certain actions (e.g. the wallpapering) and objects (e.g. the bicycle) to attain a significance beyond their immediate context.

It is also important to suggest the areas of ambiguity in the two characters: in the woman, between 'Norma Elliot', the vulnerable and passionate human being, and 'Mrs. Elliot', the implacable wife, completely committed to the standards brainwashed into her; and in the man, between the 'social catalyst' (as he sees himself), and the pub orator and permanent adolescent forever justifying his own sexual capriciousness (as she certainly sees him).

In the Royal Court production there was one interval, between Acts II and III. Photographs of working-class weddings and suburban family life were flashed on to a screen between Acts I and II. Each Act was preceded by popular music appropriate to the period of the Act.

E. A. WHITEHEAD

Act One: 1000 Women

Scene: Winter, 1962. The time is about 11.15 p.m. A lounge. MRS.
ELLIOT *is decorating. She wears a scarf round her head and a pair of
overalls.*

*She is putting new white wallpaper over the old faded orange and
has nearly finished the room. She has already painted the ceiling and
the woodwork white.*

*Decorating materials and equipment are spread across the floor,
which has been protected with newspapers, and the furniture is all
stacked to one side. She hears* MR. ELLIOT *and hurries.*

MR. ELLIOT *comes in. He is dressed smartly but in a very conserva-
tive style—belted raincoat, navy blue suit and tie, white shirt, black
shoes. He pushes his way in, looks around. Then, in silence, ignoring*
MRS. ELLIOT's *glance, he picks his way delicately through the equipment and goes into the kitchen and shuts the door.*

MRS. ELLIOT *looks after him, then resumes her work. She works
very competently and seems engrossed in it.*

After a moment MR. ELLIOT *returns with a coffee. He studies the
furniture. Parks himself on the corner of a chair, rather awkwardly.*
MRS. ELLIOT *turns round to look at him. He ignores her and scrutinizes
the room. She smiles, speaks lightly:*

MRS. ELLIOT: Thank you . . . I would like a coffee . . .
MR. ELLIOT: What?
MRS. ELLIOT: Yes . . . I would like a coffee.
MR. ELLIOT: Do you have to have a coffee just because I'm having
    a coffee?
MRS. ELLIOT: I just *feel* like a coffee . . .
MR. ELLIOT: As soon as *I* have a coffee you just feel like a coffee?

13

MRS. ELLIOT: Yes!

MR. ELLIOT: What do you feel like when I have a crap?
   (*Silence.*)

MRS. ELLIOT: I've been a very good girl today . . . worked from
   dawn to dusk.

MR. ELLIOT: Dawn to dawn, you mean.

MRS. ELLIOT: It'll soon be finished. (*Pause.*) It'll look nice when
   it's finished.
   (*Silence.* MR. ELLIOT *surveys the room.*)

MR. ELLIOT: You don't think . . .

MRS. ELLIOT: What?

MR. ELLIOT: You don't think it suffers from a certain . . .
   monotony?

MRS. ELLIOT: Monotony?

MR. ELLIOT: All this white?

MRS. ELLIOT: Oh . . . I don't know. No. I think it'll look nice . . .

MR. ELLIOT: When it's finished?

MRS. ELLIOT: Yes.

MR. ELLIOT: At least it will look newly decorated.

MRS. ELLIOT: You must admit it was ready for it.

MR. ELLIOT: I wouldn't dispute that.
   (*Silence.* MRS. ELLIOT *turns to resume work. She stops when*
   MR. ELLIOT *speaks.*)
   I see you've repaired the fence, too.

MRS. ELLIOT: What?

MR. ELLIOT: You've repaired the fence in the road.

MRS. ELLIOT: Oh . . . that. Yes. It didn't take long. (*Pause.*) I've
   only fixed it with wire . . .

MR. ELLIOT: Very enterprising.

MRS. ELLIOT: You don't . . . mind, do you?

MR. ELLIOT: Mind?

MRS. ELLIOT: About me repairing the fence?

MR. ELLIOT: No doubt the neighbours will admire your initiative.
   (*Silence.*)
   Don't let me interrupt your work.
   (MRS. ELLIOT *resumes work.*)
   (MR. ELLIOT *inspects his paperback books, re-stacks them. Then
   he settles back, sips his coffee. He studies his watch.*)

MRS. ELLIOT: Why don't you go to bed?

MR. ELLIOT: I'm not tired.

MRS. ELLIOT: Oh . . .

(*Silence.*)

Have you had anything to eat?

MR. ELLIOT: No.

MRS. ELLIOT: I'll make a snack . . . when I've done this bit.

MR. ELLIOT: I don't want anything to eat.

MRS. ELLIOT: Did you have a drink?

MR. ELLIOT: What?

MRS. ELLIOT: Did you . . . have a drink?

MR. ELLIOT: Yes!

(MR. ELLIOT *sits staring at his watch.*)

(MRS. ELLIOT *turns away as if to work. Looks at the wall.*)

In half an hour I'll be twenty-nine.

MRS. ELLIOT (*light*): We'll open a tin of sardines and celebrate!

MR. ELLIOT (*moody*): In twelve months and half an hour I'll be thirty. (*Pause.*) Christ.

(MRS. ELLIOT *hastens to finish the wallpapering.*)

MRS. ELLIOT: Where did you go?

MR. ELLIOT: What?

MRS. ELLIOT: Where did you go . . . for a drink?

MR. ELLIOT: The Basnett Bar. (*Pause.*) The others went on to a club.

MRS. ELLIOT: Oh . . .

MR. ELLIOT: With Billy.

MRS. ELLIOT: Billy?

MR. ELLIOT: We met him at the beach once with his wife. Remember? She was a tall dark girl . . . very attractive.

MRS. ELLIOT: Oh . . . I remember. With a little baby? A baby girl . . .

MR. ELLIOT: That's right.

MRS. ELLIOT: I remember.

MR. ELLIOT: He buried her a week ago.

MRS. ELLIOT: Oh . . . who?

MR. ELLIOT: His wife.

MRS. ELLIOT: She was . . . very young . . . wasn't she?

MR. ELLIOT: You mean young to die?

MRS. ELLIOT: Yes.

MR. ELLIOT (*flip*): You're never too young to die.

MRS. ELLIOT: What happened?

MR. ELLIOT: She went into hospital a year ago with a lump on her breast. They cut the lump out. Then after a few months she went back in and they cut the breast off. Then, after a little more time, she went back and they diagnosed cancer of the stomach. Inoperable. She died the week before last.

MRS. ELLIOT: Oh . . . isn't that . . . horrible . . .

MR. ELLIOT: We haven't seen Billy for a few months now. (*Pause.*) Anyway, he turned up tonight again.

MRS. ELLIOT: How was he?

MR. ELLIOT: I asked him that very question. I was wondering how he was getting on . . . how he was managing with the kids, and so on . . . and when we were on our own for a minute—standing in the bog, actually—I said to him: 'I heard about your wife.' He hadn't spoken about it to us. Anyway, I said I was sorry, and he said: 'Oh . . . yes.' So then I said: 'How are you getting on?' And he said: 'I feel like a fifteen-year-old! I'm having the time of my fucking life!'

MRS. ELLIOT: He's probably still affected by shock.

MR. ELLIOT: You *would* say that.

MRS. ELLIOT: Well . . . he may be!

MR. ELLIOT: Yeah . . . the shock of freedom.

(MRS. ELLIOT *turns grimly to her work.* MR. ELLIOT *hangs his coat in the hall and takes a paperback from the pocket.*)

MRS. ELLIOT: Who else was there?

MR. ELLIOT: Oh . . . Harry, Jim, the usual crowd.

MRS. ELLIOT: And did they go on to the club?

MR. ELLIOT: Well . . . some of them.

MRS. ELLIOT: Huh. . . . It's pathetic!

MR. ELLIOT: Don't start that . . .

MRS. ELLIOT: What?

MR. ELLIOT: All that stuff about mutton dressed as ram.

(*He comes back in. Takes some money from a pay packet and slips it into an exercise book.*)

MRS. ELLIOT: It *is* pathetic. (*Pause.*) And what . . . what stopped you?

MR. ELLIOT: I don't know. (*Pause.*) I wasn't in the mood.

MRS. ELLIOT: The mood for what?

MR. ELLIOT (*flat*): Adventure.

   (*He throws away the pay packet and puts the remaining money in his pocket.*)

MRS. ELLIOT: Huh!

MR. ELLIOT: No . . . my birthday had set me thinking . . .

MRS. ELLIOT: Looking back over the years of waste?

MR. ELLIOT: Looking forward over the years of waste.

MRS. ELLIOT: That's . . . up to you . . .

MR. ELLIOT: What's up to me? I'm a man who's about-to-be-twenty-nine . . . and next year I shall be a man-who's-about-to-be-thirty . . . and after that I shall be a man who's about-to-be-forty. I feel toothless and superseded. (*Laughs.*) Christ . . . I feel that if I paid a compliment to a pretty girl she'd assume I *wasn't* making a pass!

MRS. ELLIOT: Of course you want to pay compliments to pretty girls.

MR. ELLIOT: Of course.

MRS. ELLIOT: I think you, and your crowd, are completely pathetic . . . running round the clubs like a gang of teenagers, when every one of you has a wife . . . and a family.

MR. ELLIOT: The teenagers don't *have* to run round the clubs. (*Silence.* MRS. ELLIOT *is finishing off the wall.*)

   We had a very interesting debate tonight.

MRS. ELLIOT: Did you?

MR. ELLIOT: About the quality of working-class morality. Most of the crowd—who have of course now assumed middle-class status—agreed that working-class morality was loose and depraving: I argued that it was rigid and depraving.

MRS. ELLIOT: Depraving?

MR. ELLIOT: Yes, because it's a stallion-style morality. . . . The principle is very simple: the male pokes everything he can get until one day he inadvertently pokes himself into wedlock; after that he stops poking and starts lusting. The morality is rigid because, once married, the male never actually pokes anything else; and it's depraved because he lusts his life away in masculine obscenities and dirty jokes.

MRS. ELLIOT: WHOOPS!

(MRS. ELLIOT *struggles to secure a strip of paper that is peeling from the ceiling. She stands on a ladder to press it back.*)

(MR. ELLIOT *sits watching.*)

(*She climbs down.*)

My arms are aching . . .

(*She goes out for a coffee.*)

MR. ELLIOT (*calls*): Do you agree?

MRS. ELLIOT (*calls*): D'you want a coffee?

(MR. ELLIOT *lights a cigarette, looking impatient.*)

MR. ELLIOT: Do you agree with my views of working-class morality?

(MRS. ELLIOT *returns with two coffees. She puts one down by* MR. ELLIOT, *and perches on a chair with the other.*)

MRS. ELLIOT: Is that your morality?

MR. ELLIOT: Yes. It's a pity I can never remember dirty jokes.

MRS. ELLIOT: What did Harry think?

MR. ELLIOT: About what?

MRS. ELLIOT: Working-class morality . . .

MR. ELLIOT: He thought it was rigid and *not* depraving.

MRS. ELLIOT: Did he go to the club?

MR. ELLIOT: No.

MRS. ELLIOT: I agree with him.

MR. ELLIOT: About what?

MRS. ELLIOT: Working-class morality.

(MR. ELLIOT *stares at her in exaggerated astonishment.*)

MR. ELLIOT: *You* agree with him!

MRS. ELLIOT (*defensive*): Yes . . . I do . . .

MR. ELLIOT (*ironic*): I'm sure your father would be delighted to hear that.

(*Pause.*)

MRS. ELLIOT: My father?

MR. ELLIOT: Yes.

MRS. ELLIOT: I don't see what he has to do with it.

MR. ELLIOT: He's a classic example of what I mean about
    working-class morality.
    (*Pause.*)
MRS. ELLIOT: How is he?
MR. ELLIOT: You're always ranting on about how unfair he is to
    your mother . . . gives her a dog's life, you say. (*Pause.*)
    You said he was the soul of generosity in the alehouse and a
    monster of meanness at home.
MRS. ELLIOT: What's that got to do with . . . sexual morality?
    He's never played around . . .
MR. ELLIOT: Precisely! That's why he's a classical example!
MRS. ELLIOT: Why?
MR. ELLIOT: He only really comes alive in the company of his
    alehouse cronies. You ought to hear him with them.
MRS. ELLIOT: What ought I to hear?
MR. ELLIOT (*teasing*): Or perhaps you ought not to hear it.
MRS. ELLIOT: Hear what?
MR. ELLIOT: His jokes.
MRS. ELLIOT: What jokes?
MR. ELLIOT: As I said, I have a very poor memory.
MRS. ELLIOT: You mean dirty jokes.
    (*Silence.*)
    You mean dirty jokes, don't you?
MR. ELLIOT: Yes.
MRS. ELLIOT (*heated*): I don't believe it.
MR. ELLIOT: I laugh, of course.
MRS. ELLIOT: I bet you howl.
MR. ELLIOT: No . . . no, I don't howl. . . . (*Judiciously.*) I curl
    my lips and laugh.
MRS. ELLIOT (*contemptuously*): I bet you do.
MR. ELLIOT: Actually I feel more like puking.
MRS. ELLIOT: I don't believe you . . . about the jokes.
MR. ELLIOT: I'm not . . . attacking your father.
MRS. ELLIOT: HUH!
MR. ELLIOT: I mean . . . they all do it. They all rival each other
    in the dirtiness of their jokes. Basically, they vent their
    hatred of women through the jokes. They mock their own
    dependence on women and feel stronger for it. The more

the jokes degrade women, the more they like it, and the more they laugh. (*Pause*.) Your father's no exception.

MRS. ELLIOT: It's sickening.

MR. ELLIOT: If the men didn't tell jokes they'd probably beat the women up.

MRS. ELLIOT: Sickening . . . especially when I think of how he treated me.

MR. ELLIOT (*curious*): Treated you?

MRS. ELLIOT: He was a tyrant. Even when I was in my teens, he insisted on my being back in the house every night by nine o'clock! Nine o'clock . . . although he was never back in until well after the pubs shut, naturally. (*Pause*.) And when he did come back in . . . he'd conduct a detailed interrogation as to where I'd been, who with, what I'd done or hadn't done . . .

MR. ELLIOT: He was protecting you from your libidinous teenage impulses.

MRS. ELLIOT: He didn't need to.

MR. ELLIOT (*ironic*): You . . . didn't have any libidinous teenage impulses?

MRS. ELLIOT: I didn't need any protection.

MR. ELLIOT: What? No lustful gallants eager to give you your first experience? Your first tender, never-to-be-forgotten grope?

MRS. ELLIOT (*contemptuous*): There's never any shortage of 'lustful gallants'.

MR. ELLIOT (*pompous*): I should hope not!
(*Silence*.)
(*Serious tone*.) I suppose, what it was with your old man was that . . . having got your mother 'into trouble', as they say, over you . . . he wanted to make sure that he didn't allow the same to happen to you.

MRS. ELLIOT (*puzzled*): 'Over me'?

MR. ELLIOT: Yes.
(*Silence*.)

MRS. ELLIOT: Do you mean what you appear to mean?

MR. ELLIOT: Yes.

MRS. ELLIOT: You're going too far.

MR. ELLIOT (*sincere tone*): He told me.

MRS. ELLIOT (*cynical*): He told you what?

MR. ELLIOT: He told me that when he got married, he *had* to . . . because his wife already had a bun in the oven. That bun was you.

MRS. ELLIOT: I don't believe you.

MR. ELLIOT: Ask him.

MRS. ELLIOT: I'll do better than that—I'll ask her.

MR. ELLIOT (*reflective*): Though . . . for myself . . . I'd certainly prefer to believe that I was conceived in some wild and furtive fuck than in the routine copulations of marriage.

MRS. ELLIOT: It's romantic to think so, but you probably were.

MR. ELLIOT (*smiles*): I like to think so. (*Pause.*) It's odd, come to think of it, that we *didn't* have the usual pressing reason for wedlock, did we? Why the hell did we get married?

MRS. ELLIOT: You wanted to.

MR. ELLIOT: Didn't you?

MRS. ELLIOT: Yes. No.

MR. ELLIOT: What?

MRS. ELLIOT: I didn't really want to . . .

MR. ELLIOT: You wanted to escape from your father.

MRS. ELLIOT (*cynical*): Escape . . . to what?

MR. ELLIOT (*hand on heart*): ME!

MRS. ELLIOT: Huh! Prince Charming!

MR. ELLIOT (*romantic*): Yes . . . there you were, trapped in the ogre's castle . . . when one day, I came galloping by and swept you off your feet and . . . and then we got married and lived miserably ever after. That's the new conclusion, that, to the old fairy tale. (*Then bitterly.*) You were *desperate* to get married . . . when I met you.

MRS. ELLIOT (*cool*): You weren't the only Prince Charming around.

MR. ELLIOT (*savage*): If I hadn't married you, you would have ended up a grey-haired virgin!

MRS. ELLIOT: That's one thing I regret . . .

MR. ELLIOT: Eh?

MRS. ELLIOT: I 'saved' myself.

MR. ELLIOT (*mock shock*): I beg your pardon?

MRS. ELLIOT: I 'saved' myself. (*Laughs derisively*.) For you!
What a joke!
(MR. ELLIOT *glances sourly at her*.)
For a long time, for years in fact . . . before I met you . . .
I was courting a man that I was very fond of . . . but I
wouldn't let him touch me. (*Laughs*.) Huh! I wouldn't let
him anywhere near me.

MR. ELLIOT: Your father evidently did a very good job.

MRS. ELLIOT (*wry, sad*): Yes . . .

MR. ELLIOT: And so this man that you were fond of . . .

MRS. ELLIOT: Yes.

MR. ELLIOT (*brutal*): And so he dumped you?

MRS. ELLIOT (*level*): More or less.

MR. ELLIOT: THE BOUNDER!

MRS. ELLIOT: He was twice the man you are.

MR. ELLIOT: Naturally, now he's gone.

MRS. ELLIOT: I wasn't ready to marry him . . . but I could have
given him that.

MR. ELLIOT: You make it sound like a Christmas present.

MRS. ELLIOT: It was hardly worth 'saving' for you, anyway, was
it?

MR. ELLIOT: Me? I didn't ask you to save it.

MRS. ELLIOT (*laughs*): You wouldn't marry anyone who wasn't a
virgin. You're one of the very worst cases of the working-
class morality you've been attacking. . . . You were infected
at an early age and I doubt if you'll ever recover. You're
. . . You're a real pillar of morality.

MR. ELLIOT: I'm a pillar of the *new* morality.

MRS. ELLIOT: You really are a classic example of the working-
class buck. You don't come in rotten drunk——

MR. ELLIOT: —because I can hold my ale.

MRS. ELLIOT: —and you don't throw your dinner on the floor
like my father sometimes did——

MR. ELLIOT: —because I don't get any dinner.

MRS. ELLIOT: You could do!

MR. ELLIOT: Oh, no, oh no. We agreed, after a long succession of
incinerated dinners, that if I didn't get in before nine
o'clock, I should get no dinner. Which suits me fine, since

it removes your only excuse for attacking me when—as always—I come home after nine.

MRS. ELLIOT: . . . you *don't* swear at the children and you *don't* beat me up . . .

MR. ELLIOT: I'm beginning to feel quite saintly!

MRS. ELLIOT: . . . But essentially, you're no different from my father. (*Pause.*) Worse, in fact.

MR. ELLIOT (*mock shock*): Worse?

MRS. ELLIOT: You couldn't call my father unfaithful.

MR. ELLIOT: I didn't call your father unfaithful.

MRS. ELLIOT: No.

(*Silence.*)

MR. ELLIOT: You think I am unfaithful?

MRS. ELLIOT: Aren't you?

MR. ELLIOT: No such luck.

MRS. ELLIOT: Huh.

(*Pause.*)

MR. ELLIOT: I have not been unfaithful.

MRS. ELLIOT: For lack of opportunity?

MR. ELLIOT: Yes. (*Pause; he reflects.*) Well, to put it more precisely, for lack of courage to create the opportunity or to exploit the opportunity when offered.

MRS. ELLIOT: A faithful coward?

MR. ELLIOT: Yes.

MRS. ELLIOT: What are you afraid of then?

MR. ELLIOT: I'm afraid of being thought a dirty old man.

MRS. ELLIOT: Which you are . . .

MR. ELLIOT: Only in . . . my secret wishes. (*Whispers.*) It's our secret! Nobody knows . . . except you and me!
(MR. ELLIOT *puts his finger to his lips; picks up newspaper.*
MRS. ELLIOT *busies herself tidying up. She stops.*)

MRS. ELLIOT: Would you?

MR. ELLIOT: Would I what?

(*Pause.* MRS. ELLIOT *forces herself to speak.*)

MRS. ELLIOT: Fuck someone?

(MR. ELLIOT *reflects.*)

MR. ELLIOT: Present company excluded?

MRS. ELLIOT: There's no danger of that!

MR. ELLIOT: I wouldn't touch *you* with a bargepole, of course.
MRS. ELLIOT: You won't be offered the opportunity.
MR. ELLIOT: Fine.
MRS. ELLIOT: But you *would* fuck someone else?
    (*Silence.* MR. ELLIOT *reflects. She stares at him.*)
MR. ELLIOT: I suppose . . . speaking hypothetically, of course . . .
it is conceivable that if I were caught in the right mood . . .
if, for instance, I were relaxing at a party . . . and I saw this
angelic young dolly across the room. . . . And she was
looking at me . . . *gazing* at me, with an expression of
rapture in her peerless eyes . . . and she wandered across to
me, and addressed herself to me, and attached herself to
me. . . . And plied me with drinks and innocent flattery . . .
and lured me upstairs to some remote bedroom . . . and
there. . . . And there she turned to me with radiant face,
parted lips, melting eyes and heaving breast . . . and
unbuttoned her dress with trembling fingers. . . . And drew
me down on to the bed, and stroked my hair, and
whispered in my ear, murmuring her demure desire and
then stuffed her tit in my mouth and her hand down my
trousers. . . . (*Pause, then brisk.*) I believe I might succumb.
Yes . . . I might well concede the day there, and might
even concede the night.
    (MRS. ELLIOT *continues busily tidying up.*)
MRS. ELLIOT (*disgustedly*): You *are* sick.
MR. ELLIOT: Because I voiced a normal masculine fantasy?
MRS. ELLIOT: Because you feel it.
MR. ELLIOT: We're trained to feel it, aren't we? From the cradle?
Right through adolescence we're encouraged to cultivate our
erotic fantasies, to compete in sexual prowess . . . we're
constantly nudged by sexual innuendo and edged toward
the marriage bed . . . and then . . . and then what happens?
The women preoccupy themselves with home-making and
child-rearing and the men find consolation in fantasy. . . .
As I said, the old ones vent their frustrations in dirty jokes.
MRS. ELLIOT: And the young ones go to the clubs?
MR. ELLIOT: Yes . . . but only to look.
MRS. ELLIOT: Are they cowards too?

MR. ELLIOT: They're faithful.

MRS. ELLIOT: Like you.

(*Pause.* MR. ELLIOT *wipes his nose with a handkerchief.*)

MR. ELLIOT: You don't believe me, do you?

MRS. ELLIOT: Huh.

MR. ELLIOT: If we discount the odd bit of self-abuse, and I
assume that I am allowed to abuse *myself* if nobody else, I
have been faithful to you in my rather reluctant fashion.
(*Pause. Then grim.*)
My problem is that I am not content to look. (*Pause.*) I
don't want to turn into a voyeur.
(*Pause.* MRS. ELLIOT *starts cleaning up.*)
Did I tell you that the boys have clubbed together to buy a
film projector and they meet once a week to watch blue
movies?

MRS. ELLIOT (*stops working, stares*): Blue movies?

MR. ELLIOT (*explanatory*): Sex films.

MRS. ELLIOT: I didn't think you meant weepies. I know what
they are.

MR. ELLIOT: Oh really?

MRS. ELLIOT: Who goes?

MR. ELLIOT: They all go.

MRS. ELLIOT: Do you?

MR. ELLIOT: I've been twice.

MRS. ELLIOT: Do you enjoy them?

MR. ELLIOT: No.

MRS. ELLIOT: Why? Why not? Aren't the films sexy enough?

MR. ELLIOT: I don't mind the films. I don't like the company.

MRS. ELLIOT: I thought they were your friends?

MR. ELLIOT: They are . . . individually. But I don't like the
'all-boys-together' atmosphere. (*Pause.*) It's like the whole
First Eleven sitting masturbating in the locker room.
(*Pause.*) I'd prefer a mixed audience but they won't dream
of it.

MRS. ELLIOT: Mixed? What . . . have a few girls along and an
orgy to follow?

MR. ELLIOT (*laughs*): That's an idea. But . . . no, I think a mixed
audience would be healthier.

MRS. ELLIOT (*disbelieving*): Healthier?

MR. ELLIOT: Yes, healthier.

MRS. ELLIOT: Why?

MR. ELLIOT (*impatient*): It's all tied up with what I was saying
before . . . the masculinity bit . . . the furtive voyeurism . . .
the morality of the Northern Hero. (*Pause.*) They're all
faithful. By Christ they're faithful!
(*Silence.*)

MRS. ELLIOT: Where do they meet . . . to see the films?

MR. ELLIOT: Harry's.

MRS. ELLIOT (*amazed*): What?

MR. ELLIOT: Harry's house.
(*Silence.*)

MRS. ELLIOT: What about his wife?

MR. ELLIOT: She goes to her mother's.

MRS. ELLIOT: Does she know?

MR. ELLIOT: That's why she goes to her mother's. (*Silence.*) Do
you mind my going?

MRS. ELLIOT: You can do what you like.
(MRS. ELLIOT *finishes tidying up. She looks round the room,
pats down part of the wallpaper, surveys it again.*)
I think it'll look nice when everything's back in place.
(MR. ELLIOT *grunts.*)
I think I'll go to bed. (*Pause.*) There's some cheese there if
you want a sandwich.
(MR. ELLIOT *doesn't reply. She moves toward the door. Then
she goes into the kitchen and takes two parcels from the
cupboard. She comes back in. Holds them up.*)
Happy Birthday.

MR. ELLIOT: Huh.

MRS. ELLIOT: They're going to surprise you in the morning.

MR. ELLIOT (*heavy*): Tony's going to surprise me with a shaving
mirror and Sarah's going to surprise me with a scarf.

MRS. ELLIOT: You know?

MR. ELLIOT: They've been going on about it for weeks!

MRS. ELLIOT: They've been looking forward to it for weeks.
(*She puts the parcels down on the table and moves to the door
to go.*)

MR. ELLIOT: I think it would be healthier if we separated.

MRS. ELLIOT: What?

MR. ELLIOT: I think we ought to separate.

(MRS. ELLIOT, *stunned, moves near the wallpaper.*)

I don't suppose you remember the agreement we had . . . before we got married . . . that if ever either of us decided it had been a mistake to marry, we could always separate and then arrange a divorce?

(MRS. ELLIOT *stares in silence.*)

Do you remember that agreement?

MRS. ELLIOT: That was if there was only you and me.

MR. ELLIOT: What?

MRS. ELLIOT: Now we've got the children to think of . . .

MR. ELLIOT: That was the agreement we made about marriage.

MRS. ELLIOT: And then we had the children . . .

MR. ELLIOT: What about the agreement?

MRS. ELLIOT: That doesn't apply!

MR. ELLIOT: It applies as much as ever!

MRS. ELLIOT: Not with the children!

MR. ELLIOT: You never mentioned children.

MRS. ELLIOT: Neither did you.

MR. ELLIOT: Christ. . . . First you blackmailed me, now you're trapping me.

MRS. ELLIOT (*indignant*): Blackmailed?

MR. ELLIOT: Yes . . . as you well know.

MRS. ELLIOT: You made your own decision.

MR. ELLIOT: Even after we made that agreement . . . I was still reluctant. And when I suggested that we leave it for a year or so, until we knew each other better . . . before committing ourselves . . . when I suggested that, you threatened to commit suicide.

MRS. ELLIOT: I did hell!

MR. ELLIOT (*strained*): You said . . . quite simply . . . that if I didn't go through with the marriage you would kill yourself.

MRS. ELLIOT: I did not!

MR. ELLIOT: I remember the day you said it.

MRS. ELLIOT: YOU LYING GET!

(*Silence.*)

MR. ELLIOT: As a matter of fact I remember talking it over with Harry. I asked his advice. I remember asking him whether he thought a suicide threat would form a good foundation for a happy and lasting relationship. (*Pause.*) He seemed a bit dubious.

MRS. ELLIOT: Oh . . . did he?

MR. ELLIOT: Yes . . . but he wouldn't commit himself.

MRS. ELLIOT: Wouldn't he?

MR. ELLIOT: I suppose it was a bit much to ask.
(*Silence.*)

MRS. ELLIOT: You've come out with some lies tonight . . . about my father and his jokes . . . and my birth . . . and your being faithful . . . and the blue films . . . but now . . . now you're excelling yourself!

MR. ELLIOT: You prefer not to remember?

MRS. ELLIOT (*high-pitched*): It didn't happen!

MR. ELLIOT: It was about ten days before we were due to get married. I distinctly remember talking it over with Harry.

MRS. ELLIOT: I'll ask him!

MR. ELLIOT: Go ahead.

MRS. ELLIOT: You lying bastard.

MR. ELLIOT: I don't need to lie about that . . .

MRS. ELLIOT: I *will* ask him . . .

MR. ELLIOT: That's up to you.
(MRS. ELLIOT *goes to the telephone. She throws books aside and looks through an address book by the phone.*)
He's probably in bed now.

MRS. ELLIOT: Then I'll get him up.

MR. ELLIOT: That'll please him.

MRS. ELLIOT (*sobbing*): I'm *sick* of your lies . . .

MR. ELLIOT: Why don't you ask him tomorrow?

MRS. ELLIOT (*shrill*): I'M ASKING HIM NOW!
(MR. ELLIOT *shrugs, looks away. Picks up the poperbacks.*)
(MRS. ELLIOT *kneels by the phone with the book. Dials. The answer is immediate.* MR. ELLIOT *glances at her as she speaks.*)
Oh hello . . . Harry . . . Harry . . . this is Norma . . . Norma Elliot . . . I'm sorry it's so late . . . but . . .
(*Sobbing.*) . . . Frank and I . . . Frank and I . . . we've been

talking . . . about before we . . . er . . . before we got
married and, Frank . . . I'm sorry . . . yes, before we got
married. . . . Yes, I KNOW IT'S HIS BIRTHDAY! All
right, I'll tell him, yes, I'll tell him about the card, all
right, never mind . . . GOD! (*Pause.*) It's all right . . . I'm
a bit . . . yes . . . Frank says I threatened to commit suicide
if he didn't go through with the marriage and he says he
talked it over with you a few days before the marriage—do
you remember? Do you remember him saying that, Harry?
(*Sobbing.*) He says I said I was going to kill myself unless
. . . what? (*Pause.*) You don't? No . . . no . . . I didn't say
it . . . I didn't say anything like that. . . . No, that's all
right . . . I'm sorry . . . it's all right . . .
(MR. ELLIOT *looks at her from across the room.*)

MR. ELLIOT: All right . . . he doesn't remember.

MRS. ELLIOT: He didn't say that.

MR. ELLIOT: Eh?

MRS. ELLIOT (*shrieks*): He said it never happened!

MR. ELLIOT: He didn't want to upset you.

MRS. ELLIOT: You lying bastard!

MR. ELLIOT: I am not lying.

MRS. ELLIOT: You're always lying!

MR. ELLIOT (*violent*): I'm trying to be honest! Christ, this is
driving me nuts. I'm sick of it. All the bloody hypocrisy
and the lies and the agonies . . . I'm sick of them! I'm sick
of fantasy . . . I want reality!

MRS. ELLIOT (*sarcastic*): Reality! What reality?

MR. ELLIOT (*desperately*): I have to get out of this trap. I can't
stand it. I want to live, to grow, to stretch, to thrive . . . I
want to be free!

MRS. ELLIOT: Free for what?

MR. ELLIOT: I want to fuck a thousand women!
(MR. ELLIOT *stares furiously around the room. Turns toward the
wallpaper.*)
This house . . . it's dead. There's no life in it, no life at all.
And this room . . . white, all white . . . it's all cold and
sterile and lifeless! There's no love in this room or in this
house. NO LOVE! It's DEAD!

(MR. ELLIOT *plucks at a little strip of wallpaper that is hanging loose. It peels away, slowly, in his hand. He stares at it fascinated as it peels away. Then he suddenly tears at it and the whole strip peels off the wall, revealing the orange paper underneath. As if berserk, he tears at the next strip.*)

(MRS. ELLIOT *tries to stop him but he pushes her away and tears at the wallpaper, shouting 'DEAD DEAD DEAD!'*)

(MRS. ELLIOT *leans sobbing exhausted against the table. Then she takes the parcels and goes toward the door. MR. ELLIOT stops and looks at her.*)

(*Shouts.*) I hate this house and I hate you and I hate the brats!

(*He seizes the parcels. One contains a shaving mirror. He hurls it to the floor and stamps on it.*)

MRS. ELLIOT (*crying*): The presents! Stop it! Oh God . . . you're insane! You're insane!

(*She tries to stop him then she rushes upstairs. MR. ELLIOT follows to the door.*)

MR. ELLIOT (*shouts after her*): I hate the brats and I hate you!

(*He comes back in. He stamps again on the mirror, then tears open the parcel containing the scarf. He goes to tear the scarf, then lets it slip to the floor. He stares at it, then suddenly moans and sobs. He pulls out a handkerchief and cries.*)

CURTAIN

Act Two: Pseudomorph

Scene: Late Saturday morning in Spring, 1966. The lounge is full of sunshine. There is now a bookcase crammed with books.

MR. ELLIOT *is heard singing upstairs.*

MRS. ELLIOT *steps from the kitchen and listens. She looks as if she has been crying but is now building up an angry mood. She goes back into the kitchen.*

MR. ELLIOT *comes downstairs into the lounge. He is wearing sky blue flared slacks and his pyjama jacket. He has just had a bath and is rubbing his hair with a towel. He sings loudly, with frequent trills and flourishes:*

MR. ELLIOT: 'O, O, Antonio,
              He's gone away,
              Left me on my own-io,
              All on my own, you know,
              I'd like to catch him,
              With his new sweetheart,
              And up would go Antonio
              And his ice-cream cart!'

(*He stands in front of a wall mirror and combs his hair, experimenting with various styles: flat back like Valentino (he particularly admires this), flat forward over his eyes, centre parted like an old footballer, and completely free and uncombed . . .*)

(MRS. ELLIOT *steps from the kitchen and watches him sourly.*)

(MR. ELLIOT *prances before the mirror, in high spirits, squinting at his profile, winking archly at himself, laughing.*)

(MRS. ELLIOT *steps forward. She is holding a wet frying-pan.*

MR. ELLIOT *sees her in the mirror. He laughs and speaks into the mirror.*)
What is it? Breakfast or battery?
(MRS. ELLIOT *steps toward him. He laughs but moves away.*)
You wouldn't attack a man in his pyjamas?

MRS. ELLIOT: Where did *you* go last night?

MR. ELLIOT: Out.

MRS. ELLIOT: Where to?

MR. ELLIOT: I disremember.
(*Pause.* MRS. ELLIOT *stands staring at him angrily.*)

MRS. ELLIOT: WHERE DID YOU GET TO?

MR. ELLIOT: I went boozing and whoring around as usual.
(*Pause. He moves back to the mirror and resumes combing his hair, now serious.*)

MRS. ELLIOT: Were you with that slut?

MR. ELLIOT: Which slut?

MRS. ELLIOT: You know *which slut*!

MR. ELLIOT: You know . . . your tone is as limited as your diction. (*Pause.*) I don't know which slut. (*Then flip.*) She's just one in a thousand . . .

MRS. ELLIOT: I'll swing for her yet!

MR. ELLIOT: Nobody . . . *swings* in this civilized society.

MRS. ELLIOT: Filthy little slut!

MR. ELLIOT: Oh . . . for Christ's sake . . .
(*He stares at her in the mirror for a moment. She goes back into the kitchen. Then he combs his hair, and sings.*)
'I'd like to catch him
With his dum de da,
And up would go who you know
In his da de da!'

MRS. ELLIOT (*from kitchen*): Will you tell your slut to keep her filth out of the car?

MR. ELLIOT: Eh?

MRS. ELLIOT: Tell her to keep her filth out of the car.

MR. ELLIOT: Oh . . . what filth?

MRS. ELLIOT: HER FILTH!
(MR. ELLIOT *glances around, then back to the mirror.*)

MR. ELLIOT: O . . . O . . . Anto . . . nio . . .

(MRS. ELLIOT *comes out, goes to handbag.*)

MRS. ELLIOT: And give her this.

(MR. ELLIOT *turns.*)

(MRS. ELLIOT *flicks a small tube at him. He picks it up.*)

MR. ELLIOT: What?

MRS. ELLIOT: You know what.

MR. ELLIOT: You seem to think I'm . . . omniscient.

MRS. ELLIOT: FILTH!

MR. ELLIOT: Eyeshadow! (*Then with sad irony.*) I thought her eyes were beautiful! (*Pause. Sarcastically.*) So . . . you've been cleaning the car, have you?

MRS. ELLIOT: No . . . that's your job.

MR. ELLIOT: Oh . . .

MRS. ELLIOT: That's a job for you.

MR. ELLIOT (*a little puzzled*): Oh yes . . . we must have the family saloon polished and gleaming for this afternoon, mustn't we?

MRS. ELLIOT (*laughs*): Huh!

(MR. ELLIOT *stares at her, worried by her manner.*)

MR. ELLIOT (*straightforward*): What's so funny?

MRS. ELLIOT: You dirtied it . . . you clean it.

(MR. ELLIOT *goes through the kitchen to the garage.*)

(MRS. ELLIOT *tidies up. Put's child's bicycle in garden. Goes to kitchen.* MR. ELLIOT *storms back in.*)

MR. ELLIOT (*blustering*): Stupid bitch! What good does that do?

MRS. ELLIOT: What?

MR. ELLIOT: You've scrawled all over the car!

MRS. ELLIOT: I haven't 'scrawled all over the car' . . .

MR. ELLIOT: You've scratched the body!

MRS. ELLIOT (*vicious glee*): I wrote 'SLUT' on the bonnet.

MR. ELLIOT: . . . and scraped the paintwork. Cost a fortune to repair. You can't just . . . *wash* . . . that stuff off, you know.

MRS. ELLIOT: Leave it the way it is.

MR. ELLIOT: Yes . . . that's an idea. (*Pause.*) It'll be a bit of a diversion at School Sports Day . . . for the parents and teachers, I mean. They can while away the afternoon discussing who Mr. Elliot's slut is, and forget about their brats.

(MR. ELLIOT *sits down and hurls the towel across the room,*
just missing MRS. ELLIOT. *She picks it up.*)
(*She sits on the couch, looking at him from the side.*)
In fact, you couldn't have chosen a better way of
publicizing our . . . arrangement.

MRS. ELLIOT: *You* don't have to go to the Sports Day.

MR. ELLIOT: You've been on about it all week!

MRS. ELLIOT: We can easily walk there and back . . .

MR. ELLIOT: Throughout the week you have *repeatedly*
asseverated that the success of our brats in the athletics
depended *totally* on my inspiring presence. In fact . . . in
fact you made it clear that if I was not present then Sarah
would break her neck in the Long Jump and Tony would
set fire to the Entertainments Tent!

MRS. ELLIOT: Where do you go?

MR. ELLIOT: What?

MRS. ELLIOT: Where do you go?

MR. ELLIOT: Where do I go where?

MRS. ELLIOT: With her?

MR. ELLIOT: Oh hell . . .

MRS. ELLIOT: Where do you go? (*Voice rising.*) Do you go to . . .
the Promenade at Otterspool? (*Pause.*) Or Sefton Park?
Or is that too public? (*Pause.*) Or do you drive down behind
the warehouses in the Dock Road? (*Pause.*) Where do you
go with her?

MR. ELLIOT (*flat*): We sit and shag in the middle of Lime Street.
(*Pause.*)

MRS. ELLIOT: Are you still seeing her?

MR. ELLIOT: Who?

MRS. ELLIOT: YOU KNOW WHO!

MR. ELLIOT: You keep saying that! (*Mocking.*) 'You know who
you know who you know who . . .' I don't. I don't know!

MRS. ELLIOT: Your slut.

MR. ELLIOT (*polite inquiry*): You mean Eileen?
(*The expression of the name has a shock effect on* MRS. ELLIOT,
who trembles with anger and struggles for self-control.)
(MR. ELLIOT *sits tense but composed.*)
(*Long silence.*)

MRS. ELLIOT: It's funny . . .

MR. ELLIOT: What?

MRS. ELLIOT: All your sluts . . . (*Pause.*) Maur*een* . . . Dor*een* . . . J*ean* . . . Eil*een* . . .

MR. ELLIOT (*smiling*): Yes . . . they all share the same ending. (*He howls with laughter; then smiling.*) I made a joke . . .

MRS. ELLIOT (*sourly*): You ought to write a poem about them.

MR. ELLIOT: I could just as easily write a poem about Dora . . . Vera . . . Brenda . . . (*Pause.*) My mother was much preoccupied with names. She had them all classified. Good names like . . . Helen. Phoney names like . . . Shirley. Ugly names like Edna. (*Pause.*) It's a primitive obsession. Are you going nuts?

MRS. ELLIOT: Is that surprising?

MR. ELLIOT: You always were a bit weird.

(*Long pause.* MR. ELLIOT *moves to get up from the chair.*)

MRS. ELLIOT: I want to know.

MR. ELLIOT: What?

(*Long pause.*)

You want to know WHAT?

MRS. ELLIOT: Are you still seeing her?

MR. ELLIOT (*considered*): No.

(MRS. ELLIOT *stares hard at him from the side. He stares toward the garden.*)

MRS. ELLIOT: Swear . . .

MR. ELLIOT (*mocking: child's voice*): Cross my heart and swear to die . . .

MRS. ELLIOT (*very tense*): I want you to swear.

MR. ELLIOT (*chuckles*): All right, all right.

MRS. ELLIOT: Do you swear you're not still seeing her?

MR. ELLIOT: I swear whatever you like . . .

MRS. ELLIOT: DO YOU SWEAR? YOU'RE NOT SEEING HER?

MR. ELLIOT (*flatly*): I swear.

(*Pause.* MRS. ELLIOT *leans forward toward him.*)

MRS. ELLIOT (*disbelieving*): Swear . . . on your mother's grave?

MR. ELLIOT (*explodes*): OH! For Christ's sake!

(*He jumps up. She grabs his sleeve. He stops.*)

MRS. ELLIOT: Swear on your mother's grave . . .

MR. ELLIOT (*heavily and as if on the stand*): I swear on my mother's grave that I am not seeing her.

MRS. ELLIOT (*eagerly*): . . . Eileen . . .

(MR. ELLIOT *groans and delicately releases her hold on his sleeve, almost in slow motion.*)

MR. ELLIOT (*witness-box tone again*): I swear on my mother's grave that I am not seeing Eileen.

(MRS. ELLIOT *sits back in the couch, tight-lipped.* MR. ELLIOT *looks down at her. Silence.*)

Why . . . WHY . . . do you focus your vindictiveness on *her*? Her . . . out of a thousand? Why her?

MRS. ELLIOT: Because I know who she is.

MR. ELLIOT (*surprised*): Oh . . . you've been cleaning my suits again, have you?

MRS. ELLIOT: She'll pay . . .

MR. ELLIOT: What?

MRS. ELLIOT: She'll pay!

MR. ELLIOT (*softly*): Even if I'm not seeing her?

MRS. ELLIOT (*harsh*): Aren't you?

MR. ELLIOT: CHRIST!

(*Long pause.*)

You know . . . the real issue here . . . the real thing at issue . . . is which of us is going to go nuts first. Or rather, which of us is going to go nuts *last*. (*Laughs.*) Last to go nuts goes free!

MRS. ELLIOT: Huh . . . that's no problem. You're never going free.

MR. ELLIOT: Who wants to 'go' free? I'm free now.

MRS. ELLIOT: Are you?

MR. ELLIOT: And I'm quite satisfied with our arrangement.

(*He goes to the kitchen and brings out an ironing-board. Plugs the iron into a socket. Fetches shirts from a basket in the hall. Begins ironing.*)

(MRS. ELLIOT *sits watching.*)

(*Ironing an orange shirt. Speaks in reasonable tones but with an underlying bite.*) Our arrangement does still . . . stand, I take it? (*Pause.*) You do accept the terms we agreed . . . don't you?

(He stops and looks at MRS. ELLIOT, *who looks away. He shrugs, speaks quietly.)*

I don't mind whether I live *here* . . . or on my own, somewhere. It makes no difference to me. So . . . if you want me to live here . . . if you *still* want me to stay here with you and the kids, I'm quite willing to do so. *(Pause. Then sharp.)* As long as you don't interfere with my *private* life. *(Studies* MRS. ELLIOT: *she ignores him.)* We did agree, didn't we, that I should continue to live here, paying the mortgage and insurance bills on the property, every month . . . and the gas and electricity and telephone bills every quarter . . . and the rates every year . . . plus, of course, adequate housekeeping money every week?

MRS. ELLIOT: HUH!

MR. ELLIOT *(sour look)*: In other words, we agreed, didn't we, that I should devote my total income to the upkeep of the family, and live . . . *live* . . . on, or rather OFF, my overdraft? And of course, I should do all my own shopping and cooking and laundry? *(Pause.)* In return for which, you would not interfere with my *private* life. . . . Agreed? *(He stops and looks at* MRS. ELLIOT.) We did agree, didn't we . . .? *(She looks sourly at him.)*

On those terms we agreed to carry on with this mockery of a marriage . . . which is to say, this mockery of a mockery . . .

MRS. ELLIOT: Do you know how ridiculous you look in those trousers?

MR. ELLIOT: What?

MRS. ELLIOT: You heard.

MR. ELLIOT: My sailor pants? *(Coy.)* I think they're very fetching.

MRS. ELLIOT: All you need now is beads and sandals.

MR. ELLIOT *(light)*: And whiskers . . .
        (Pause.)

MRS. ELLIOT: You're not going dressed like that, are you?

MR. ELLIOT: Why not?

MRS. ELLIOT: At School Sports?

MR. ELLIOT: Why not?

MRS. ELLIOT (*derisive*): They'll all take you for one of the Sixth
　　Form!

MR. ELLIOT: I'll make a few schoolgirl hearts flutter . . .

MRS. ELLIOT: You'll make yourself a laughing stock!

MR. ELLIOT (*wounded*): What do you want me to wear?

MRS. ELLIOT: Anything suitable for your age . . . if you've got
　　anything.

MR. ELLIOT (*angry*): White shirt and pullover and grey flannels?

MRS. ELLIOT: Whatever you like.

MR. ELLIOT: All right, all right!
　　(*He snatches a white shirt from the pile, holds it up and begins
　　to iron, furiously.*)

MRS. ELLIOT: And when are you going to get Sarah her School
　　Uniform?

MR. ELLIOT: She doesn't *have* to have a School Uniform.

MRS. ELLIOT (*bitter*): She'll be the only child there without one
　　this afternoon. (*Pause.*) Anyway . . . you promised her one.

MR. ELLIOT: Oh . . . did I?

MRS. ELLIOT: You did . . . (*Biting.*) Eighteen months ago.

MR. ELLIOT: In that case I have broken my promise . . .

MRS. ELLIOT: Yes!

MR. ELLIOT: . . . which will confirm Sarah in the opinion of me
　　that you are carefully cultivating.

MRS. ELLIOT (*sour*): I don't *need* to cultivate it!

MR. ELLIOT: Do you ever stop to consider the effect your raving
　　has on the child? Your raving about men, in general . . .
　　and me, in particular? (*Pause.*) She'll turn queer . . .

MRS. ELLIOT: She might be better off at that.

MR. ELLIOT: Christ . . . don't tell me you're developing
　　reservations about marriage too?

MRS. ELLIOT: I always did have reservations about marriage . . .
　　(*Long silence.* MR. ELLIOT *irons away.*)
　　Was *she* a virgin?

MR. ELLIOT: Who? (*Then quickly.*) Don't say it—'my slut'!

MRS. ELLIOT: Was she?

MR. ELLIOT (*sings*): 'She said she was a virgin
　　　　　　　　　　　But alas she spoke too soon!'

MRS. ELLIOT: Sometimes I'm sorry for her. (*Pause.*) You're

really sick. You're really.   a sick, randy, adolescent Peter Pan.

MR. ELLIOT (*cheerful*): Skip the Peter—just call me Pan! (*Pause.*) Your only real grievance is that I'm randy and *successful*. (MR. ELLIOT *carries on ironing.*)
(*After a while he stops and looks at* MRS. ELLIOT.)
Why *did* you marry me then?

MRS. ELLIOT: I was sorry for you.

MR. ELLIOT: Huh!

MRS. ELLIOT: I didn't . . . really . . . want to get married. I'd seen the girls at work crowing over their brand new gold rings . . . and I'd seen them a year later, living in broken-down flats, with a baby at the breast and another on the way . . . and sick of it all. When I met you I was old enough to know the difference between a wedding and a marriage! (*Pause.*) That was why I hadn't got married . . . before. (*Pause.*) I didn't want children. I don't want children now. (*Then ironic.*) But as they say in the magazines, when you have them you love them. (*Then bitter.*) You haven't got much choice. (*Pause.*) I worry about Tony sometimes. He's got exactly the same wild, coltish quality you had . . . before you hardened.

MR. ELLIOT: ME? Hard?

MRS. ELLIOT: Yes . . . you've grown hard with people as you've grown weak with yourself. You always were weak . . . you've grown weaker.

MR. ELLIOT: And . . . like they say in the magazines . . . I suppose it was my weakness that won you?

MRS. ELLIOT: Yes.
(*Long pause.* MR. ELLIOT *returns determinedly to his ironing. Sings harshly:* 'IF ANY YOUNG LADY WANTS A BABY, COME TO THE COCK OF THE NORTH!'
(MRS. ELLIOT *stares at him for a while.*)
Do they know you're married?

MR. ELLIOT: Who?

MRS. ELLIOT: These . . . little sluts . . . you pick up in the clubs . . .

MR. ELLIOT: They can see my fingernails.

(MR. ELLIOT *goes upstairs.*)
(MRS. ELLIOT *crosses to the ironing-board and looks at the
shirts. She sits down again.*)
(MR. ELLIOT *returns with a pair of grey trousers and begins to
iron them.*)
You're not going like that, are you?

MRS. ELLIOT: Eh?

MR. ELLIOT: You're not going to Sports Day dressed like that,
are you?

MRS. ELLIOT (*a bit defensive*): Why . . .

MR. ELLIOT: You look like an old shrew.

MRS. ELLIOT: That's not surprising!

MR. ELLIOT: You don't have to *look* the part.

MRS. ELLIOT (*voice rising*): And what else have I got to wear? I
got *this* dress two years ago . . . (*Shrill.*) . . . one of my
sister's cast-offs!

MR. ELLIOT (*brutal*): That's because you're a bloody awful
housekeeper.

MRS. ELLIOT (*aghast*): WHAT?
(*She rushes to a sideboard, produces an exercise book and
pushes it in front of* MR. ELLIOT. *He refuses to look at it.*)
Last week . . . four pounds three shillings housekeeping.
Four pounds to feed a family!

MR. ELLIOT: You don't feed *me*.

MRS. ELLIOT: You use tea, and milk, and sugar . . . where do
they come from? Look at the week before . . . three pounds
eighteen!

MR. ELLIOT (*grins*): It's the end of the month.

MRS. ELLIOT: Every week's the end of the month with you!

MR. ELLIOT: You'd be better off if you let me separate.

MRS. ELLIOT: HUH! If I can't get the money when you're
here . . .

MR. ELLIOT: You'd get your money.

MRS. ELLIOT: How much do you give her?

MR. ELLIOT (*mechanical*): Who?

MRS. ELLIOT: YOUR SLUT!

MR. ELLIOT: Give her?

MRS. ELLIOT: Why else should she go with you? With an old man?

MR. ELLIOT: Because I'm sexy and handsome.

MRS. ELLIOT: HUH!

MR. ELLIOT: If you want to know, she often used to help *me* out. Because . . . often . . . I was broke. (*Pause, then bitter.*) Which is not all that surprising, considering what it costs to maintain you and the brats!

MRS. ELLIOT (*looking sourly at his clothes*): I bet they cost a few pounds.

MR. ELLIOT: Which I earned.

MRS. ELLIOT: What?

MR. ELLIOT (*hard*): They cost a few pounds . . . which I EARNED!

(*Long pause. MR. ELLIOT irons.*)

MRS. ELLIOT: You borrowed the money off your father.

(MR. ELLIOT *is surprised but ignores this. Pause.*)

You'd better pay him back, hadn't you . . . before it's too late?

MR. ELLIOT: He's not . . . on his death-bed yet, you know. (*Then heated.*) He's the only thing that keeps me here! (*Pause.*) Apart from the fact that I can't afford the price of a suitcase! (*Turns to MRS. ELLIOT.*) Why don't you get a job?

MRS. ELLIOT: What?

MR. ELLIOT: You rant on about being short of money . . . why don't you get a job?

MRS. ELLIOT: To subsidize your whoring?

MR. ELLIOT (*despairing*): Ahhhh.

(*Long pause. MR. ELLIOT stops ironing.*)

It's crazy. I owe my father money.

MRS. ELLIOT (*shrill*): You owe *me* money!

MR. ELLIOT (*heavily*): I owe *you* money. I owe my friends money. I owe my employers money. I owe the bank money. (*Pause.*) Christ, I must owe *myself* money! (*Pause; muttering to himself.*) I owe myself something, anyway. (*Pause; then, turning, points to MRS. ELLIOT.*) Why the hell do we stay together? (*She ignores him.*) You are my poison ivy, I am your wall, da de da . . . (*Pause.*) We're held together by a string of . . . mini-bonds . . . that mean precisely nothing! Why? (*Then measured.*) I think I would like a divorce after all.

MRS. ELLIOT (*quickly*): You've no grounds for divorce.

MR. ELLIOT: I've got the only grounds for divorce . . . I'm *married*! (*Pause.*) This . . . arrangement . . . of ours . . . won't work. It's a shell within a shell. And it won't work, because you won't allow it to. You say you will, but in fact you insist on . . . *hounding* me! And the hypocrisy of it is driving me nuts! (*Pause.*)

MRS. ELLIOT: I suppose you think you're in love with *her*?

MR. ELLIOT (*theatrical*): Yes! Madly! Madly in love! When she breathes in, I breathe out!

MRS. ELLIOT: But you don't see her . . .

MR. ELLIOT: *There* you go again . . . (*Pause; takes dictionary from bookshelf and points out word.*) You know . . . when a structure has lost its essence but retained its shape, the geologists call it: a Pseudomorph. A false shape. (*Pause.*) That's our marriage . . . a false shape: a Pseudomorph.

MRS. ELLIOT: Very neat.

MR. ELLIOT (*resigned*): Thank you. (*Then as if making an announcement.*) 'The marriage survived and the partners quietly withered.' Christ! I want us to look forward to a Silver Divorce! I can't live this way! (*Turns to her; harsh.*) Why can't you go out and get yourself poked by some great hairy male . . .

MRS. ELLIOT (*light*): . . . to ease your conscience?

MR. ELLIOT (*raving*): . . . to cure your obsession with me! To stop you hounding me! I'm not the man you want but you insist on trying to *make* me what you want. You want me to be a good paterfamilias and I am *not* a good paterfamilias and I don't *want* to be a good paterfamilias! I want to be . . . *me*. I don't want to be 'Mr. Elliot of Greengate Avenue' . . . I want to be me! I want to live . . . live *my* way of life. I want . . . JOY!

MRS. ELLIOT: But you *are* Mr. Elliot of Greengate Avenue . . .

MR. ELLIOT: I *hate* Mr. Elliot!

MRS. ELLIOT (*laughs*): You're mad.

MR. ELLIOT: I'm heading in that direction. (*He sits. Pause. Then pleading.*) Why can't we just agree to live separately . . . and honestly?

MRS. ELLIOT (*snaps*): I MADE YOU! She's not going to get the benefit.

MR. ELLIOT (*deep frustration*): Ahhhh.

MRS. ELLIOT: Maybe you feel trapped . . . but don't forget, I'm trapped too.

MR. ELLIOT: O.K. . . . we're both trapped. (*Pause.*) You know, it's crazy. . . . Society is organized to create loneliness . . . the loneliness that leads to marriage. Society creates the disease . . . then prescribes a worse one as cure. Men enslave women . . . then wake up to find they've enslaved themselves!
(*Pause.*)
Do we like to torture ourselves? Because that's what we've, so carefully, arranged. (*Then bitterly, incredulous.*) When I was a boy I used to chastise myself . . . in emulation of the great Catholic masochists . . . like St. John of the Cross. For three weeks I wore a rope of barbed wire round my waist . . . to mortify the flesh. But after three weeks the flesh began to scream . . . and I took the rope off. (*Pause.*) Now . . . now I wear that rope of wire around my brain . . . (*Hands to head.*) . . . it's biting deeper and deeper and deeper . . . and I *can't* get it off!
(*Long pause.*)

MRS. ELLIOT (*composed but bitter*): I'm sick of it too . . . you know.

MR. ELLIOT: Then why hang on to it?

MRS. ELLIOT (*ignoring him*): I've *grown* sick of it. I've grown sick of you, and sick of sex, and sick of love. (*Pause.*) I'm sick of all the burning and the fretting and the weeping . . . I'm sick of the betrayals and sick of the fidelity . . . I'm sick of the lies and sick of the truth. I want nothing more of it. I am sick of it all.
(*Long pause.*)

MR. ELLIOT: Then why . . . hang on to it?

MRS. ELLIOT: Because I've resigned myself to it.

MR. ELLIOT: Oh . . . have you?

MRS. ELLIOT: . . . and you'll have to resign yourself to it too.

MR. ELLIOT: If you've 'resigned' yourself to it . . . why do you hound me? (*Pause; then violently.*) And why do you hound *her*?

MRS. ELLIOT: Who?
(*Pause.*)
Hound who?
(*Long pause.*)
(*Indignant and suspicious.*) Why do I hound who?
(MR. ELLIOT *turns away and busies himself with the ironing. Silence.*)
(*Shrill.*) What did you mean by that?

MR. ELLIOT (*turns on her*): Oh . . . BUGGER OFF!
(MRS. ELLIOT *glances at him. Then, composing herself.*)

MRS. ELLIOT: I haven't been 'hounding' anyone.
(MR. ELLIOT *turns and looks at her. He is provoked but restrained.*)

MR. ELLIOT (*sarcastic*): Oh no?

MRS. ELLIOT: No.

MR. ELLIOT: Haven't you?

MRS. ELLIOT: NO!
(*Pause. MR. ELLIOT resumes ironing. Silence. Then speaking conversationally, almost indifferently.*)

MR. ELLIOT: I heard you had.

MRS. ELLIOT (*quickly*): Had what?

MR. ELLIOT: I heard you'd been hounding her.

MRS. ELLIOT: Who?

MR. ELLIOT: Eileen.

MRS. ELLIOT: Huh . . . (*Pause; then tensely.*) How did you hear that?

MR. ELLIOT (*flat*): That doesn't matter.

MRS. ELLIOT (*voice trembling a little*): How . . . did you hear?

MR. ELLIOT: I heard you'd been telephoning . . . screaming and raving on the phone. You kept calling her 'slut'. Slut slut slut . . .

MRS. ELLIOT (*agitated*): Have you been seeing her?

MR. ELLIOT: It's got to stop! You understand what I mean?
(*He turns and stands confronting MRS. ELLIOT.*)

MRS. ELLIOT: I didn't telephone!

MR. ELLIOT: Then who did?

(*Silence.*)

Somebody telephoned her at work.

(MRS. ELLIOT *stares at her hands. She is trembling.*)

MRS. ELLIOT (*shrill*): I'm going to make that little slut pay.

MR. ELLIOT (*harsh but composed*): If you try—if you even *try*—
I'll sell the house and send the kids to boarding school.

MRS. ELLIOT (*quickly*): You can't do that!

MR. ELLIOT: Can't I?

MRS. ELLIOT (*shrill*): I DIDN'T TELEPHONE!

MR. ELLIOT (*bitter*): *Somebody* telephoned. (*Pause.*) Somebody
telephoned her at work and threatened to tell her family
'what she was'.

MRS. ELLIOT: I didn't.

MR. ELLIOT: Who then? (*Pause.*) Your sister?

(*Silence. Then* MR. ELLIOT *speaks in reasonable tones,
appealing to her.*)

Look . . . I know . . . I know how——

MRS. ELLIOT: Have you been seeing her?

MR. ELLIOT: Will you listen? Her father is ill——

MRS. ELLIOT: Have you been seeing her?

MR. ELLIOT (*shouts*): YES! YES I HAVE!

MRS. ELLIOT: You lying bastard!

MR. ELLIOT (*very angry*): Her father is ill—*very* ill—and if you
start——

MRS. ELLIOT (*trembling, very shrill*): I knew! I knew you'd been
seeing her . . .

MR. ELLIOT: I'm not seeing her now. Her father is very ill——

MRS. ELLIOT: I hope he dies in agony!

(MR. ELLIOT *slaps her hard across the face. She kicks him.*)
(*He jumps back, knocking over the ironing-board, and falls
with it. As he moves to get up she screeches, kicks him again.
He falls, gets up. He tries to punch her, they grapple and
thresh round the room in a fury of blows and scratches,
knocking over furniture and swearing viciously at each other.*)
(*Finally, exhausted, they lie apart, staring at each other.* MR.
ELLIOT *leans against a chair, struggling for breath.*)

MR. ELLIOT: Oh Christ . . . we have got to end this. (*Pause.*)
This Roman Arena . . . you with your net . . . and me with

my bloody trident. . . . (*Gasps—laughs.*) And upstairs . . .
the little Emperor . . . and the Empress . . . listening . . .
turning down thumbs. . . . We have got to *end* this farce.
(*Pause; he moves to get up.*) Right. All right. We'll carry on
. . . for a bit . . . with our agreement . . . all right? And
we'll go . . . to the Sports . . . we'll play our parts this
afternoon . . .

(*As he speaks,* MRS. ELLIOT *shudders; her eyes brighten; and she
screeches wildly, piercingly and breaks into a fit of weird,
hysterical non-stop babbling that drowns his speech.*)

MRS. ELLIOT: SLUTTYSLUTTYSLUTTYSLUTTYSLUTTY
SLUTTYSLUTTYSLUTTYSLUTTYSLUTTY
SLUTTYSLUTTY

(MR. ELLIOT *stares at her, horrified and frightened as she
babbles on.*)

CURTAIN

Act Three: Alpha Beta

Scene: Summer, 1971. The lounge. Very untidy, poorly decorated, and the furnishing is worn. On a table is a stainless steel tray with three tumblers full of water.

The french window opens on to an overgrown garden. A child's bicycle lies on its side on the grass. It is raining. The time is about nine in the evening and the light is beginning to fade.

MRS. ELLIOT *sits motionless in an armchair. She wears a shapeless cotton dress.*

MR. ELLIOT *lets himself in the front door and enters. He wears a shiny brown suit and coat, soaked with rain. He looks tired, old and tense.*

MR. ELLIOT: Hi.
  > (MRS. ELLIOT *doesn't answer or look at him.*)
  > What's the matter?
  > (*He sits on the arm of a couch on her left. There is complete silence.*)
  > What's the matter?
  > (*Silence. He stares at her. She stares ahead.*)
  > Where are the kids? (*Pause.*) In bed?
  > (*He gets up. Looks at MRS. ELLIOT. Then he goes out and upstairs. She remains staring.*)
  > (*Re-enters, quietly. Looks relieved.*) I didn't wake them.
  > (*He stands looking at MRS. ELLIOT. She ignores him.*)
  > Is your head bad?
  > (*Her foot jerks. She ignores it. He stares at her foot. After a long pause her foot jerks again. He looks at her face but she is still staring straight ahead.*)

Fancy a cup of coffee?

(*He goes into the kitchen to make the coffee. He looks round the kitchen. It is in a mess.*)

I came as soon as I could. There was a bit of a crisis in the office. You know . . . the announcement. Did you hear the announcement? Seems like the strike's off . . . for a day or two, anyway. So for three weeks I'm sitting there waiting for the phone to ring and today it never stops. Mind you, I half expected it. As soon as the Government said they would use troops to lift perishable cargo—that was a couple of days ago—I knew they'd have to do something. (*Pause.*) The dockers said they'd handle perishable cargo for *medical* supplies, or anything urgent like that . . .

(MR. ELLIOT *comes back in. Takes the glasses off the tray. Looks at them for a moment. Leaves them on the table and takes the tray. Speaks from the kitchen.*)

Some of the calls I've had . . . they're crazy! They think because the strike's off they'll have supplies in the shops tonight! That all I have to do is telephone a few drivers and the job's done. Deliveries under way! Perishable cargo . . . they don't know what the word means.

(MR. ELLIOT *comes back with the tray, carrying two coffees and a plate of biscuits.*)

They wouldn't thank you for fifty thousand bad bananas!

(*He puts the tray down on the floor between the couch and the armchair. Offers* MRS. ELLIOT *a cup of coffee. She ignores it. He puts it on the floor. He sits on the couch.*)

Some biscuits there. (*Pause.*) How's your head been?

MRS. ELLIOT: My head's been all right.

(*Silence.*)

MR. ELLIOT: Oh . . . good.

(MRS. ELLIOT *gets up and goes out, upstairs.* MR. ELLIOT *sips his coffee. He puts down the coffee and looks critically round the room. He looks toward the garden and sees the bike in the rain. Stands by the window and studies the state of the garden. Then looks again round the room.*)

(MRS. ELLIOT *comes back and sits in the same place.*)

All right?

MRS. ELLIOT (*sitting*): What?

MR. ELLIOT (*sitting*): The . . . the kids?

MRS. ELLIOT: I didn't look.

(*Silence.* MR. ELLIOT *studies the stainless steel tray.*)

MR. ELLIOT (*making conversation*): You've started using the tray.

MRS. ELLIOT (*staring ahead*): Mmmm.

MR. ELLIOT: It's a nice tray. Handsome.

MRS. ELLIOT (*looking at it*): We might as well use it.

MR. ELLIOT (*embarrassed*): Oh yeah . . . you might as well. It's only going . . .

MRS. ELLIOT: It was going rusty.

MR. ELLIOT: Rusty? Really? (*Picks it up and examines it.*) It was supposed to be stainless steel.

MRS. ELLIOT: They still *rust*.

MR. ELLIOT: Oh . . . yeah . . . I suppose so.

MRS. ELLIOT (*bitterly*): And it was bought two years ago.

MR. ELLIOT (*scrutinizing it*): I know.

MRS. ELLIOT: It's underneath.

MR. ELLIOT: What?

MRS. ELLIOT (*snaps*): The *rust*.

MR. ELLIOT: Oh . . . yeah . . . I see.

MRS. ELLIOT: That was why we decided to use it.

MR. ELLIOT: You've cleaned it up . . .

MRS. ELLIOT: You'd look silly giving it to your father now.

MR. ELLIOT: Now?

MRS. ELLIOT: It was supposed to be a birthday present. (*Bitterly.*) Don't you remember?

MR. ELLIOT (*guilty*): Yes.

MRS. ELLIOT: He was asking about the job. How it was going.

MR. ELLIOT (*embarrassed*): Was he?

MRS. ELLIOT: On Saturday.

MR. ELLIOT: What did you say?

MRS. ELLIOT: I said it was all right . . . as far as I knew.

MR. ELLIOT: Yeah . . . it's all right. (*Pause.*) Well . . . the dock strike didn't help. The girls were sitting in the office with nothing to do.

MRS. ELLIOT: What about you?

MR. ELLIOT: What?

MRS. ELLIOT (*dry*): Couldn't *you* keep them occupied?

MR. ELLIOT: Me? (*Pause.*) I was in the same boat. (*Laughs mirthlessly.*) I made a joke. (*Pause.*) Your coffee will be cold. (MRS. ELLIOT *very deliberately picks up the coffee and sips it.*) (*Defensive.*) How was he?

MRS. ELLIOT (*making him say it*): Who?

MR. ELLIOT: My father.

MRS. ELLIOT (*level*): He had a cold.

MR. ELLIOT (*concerned*): Oh . . .

MRS. ELLIOT: He hadn't been out for two days. He stayed in bed.

MR. ELLIOT (*approving*): Yeah . . . that was sensible. That's the best thing to do with a cold.

MRS. ELLIOT: He looks after himself.

MR. ELLIOT: He's stronger than you think.

MRS. ELLIOT (*snaps*): How would you know?

MR. ELLIOT: All I meant was . . . He's basically a *strong* man . . . sound . . . he's got a sound constitution . . . and good reserves of strength . . .

MRS. ELLIOT: He's old.

MR. ELLIOT: He's not old!

MRS. ELLIOT: What is he then?

MR. ELLIOT: He's only . . . sixty . . . (*Lamely.*) . . . sixty-seven.

MRS. ELLIOT: I suppose you think that's young?

MR. ELLIOT: Well . . . I'm not saying he's *young* . . . I mean . . . (*Pause.*) I mean, he's very strong . . . for a man of his age.

MRS. ELLIOT: You said he wasn't old.

MR. ELLIOT: O.K. . . . He's not old for a man of his age.

MRS. ELLIOT: No . . . he's a young sixty-seven.

MR. ELLIOT: Well . . . he *is*.

MRS. ELLIOT: Which still does not make him young.

MR. ELLIOT: I did not say he was *young*!

MRS. ELLIOT (*snarls*): You said he was *not old*.
(*Silence.* MR. ELLIOT *stands decisively. Pause. He stoops and puts the coffee cups on the tray. Hers is unfinished. He proffers it, she ignores him. Walks toward the kitchen. Stops by the table to put the three glasses on the tray.*)
(*Sharp.*) Leave them there.

MR. ELLIOT: What?

MRS. ELLIOT: Leave them there.

> (MR. ELLIOT *scrutinizes the glasses. Goes to take a sip.*)
> (*Snaps—warning.*) Leave it alone!

MR. ELLIOT (*puzzled and annoyed*): What is it? Lemonade?

MRS. ELLIOT: Just leave the glasses there.

MR. ELLIOT: Is it water?

MRS. ELLIOT (*hard*): Yes.

MR. ELLIOT: There's more in the tap, isn't there? It looks **untidy**. (*Sarcastic.*) Or doesn't it bother you?

MRS. ELLIOT: About as much as it bothers you.

> (MR. ELLIOT *flinches. Then he goes into the kitchen, leaving the glasses on the table.*)
> (MRS. ELLIOT *sits motionless, staring toward the garden, while he washes up.*)

MR. ELLIOT (*shouts from kitchen*): THIS KITCHEN LOOKS A DUMP!

> (*He comes back in. Starts clearing up tea table.*)
> Why don't you clean it up?

MRS. ELLIOT: Why don't you?

MR. ELLIOT: That's your job.

MRS. ELLIOT: HUH!

MR. ELLIOT: It *is* your job.

MRS. ELLIOT: It's your kitchen. You clean it up.

MR. ELLIOT: You *are* supposed to be the housewife round here, aren't you?

MRS. ELLIOT: And you're supposed to be the househusband . . . 'round here' . . . aren't you?

MR. ELLIOT: I'm not talking about that.

MRS. ELLIOT: Oh no . . . you wouldn't be!

MR. ELLIOT (*heavy control*): I'm simply referring to the fact that you have no obligations . . . no duties . . . no tasks . . . no responsibilities . . . in a word, no JOB . . . beyond that of running this household, i.e. looking after the children and maintaining the property in good order . . . and, in the circumstances, you might reasonably be expected to do more than sit on your fanny all day staring into space!

MRS. ELLIOT (*vicious mimicry*): 'Maintain the property in good order . . .'

MR. ELLIOT: Yes.

MRS. ELLIOT (*jeering*): You're more worried about the property than you are about the children!

MR. ELLIOT (*at the door*): What? What does that mean?

MRS. ELLIOT (*full flood*): You and your property! Are you worried about the price you'll get? Is that what's worrying you?

MR. ELLIOT (*baffled*): I don't get you . . .

MRS. ELLIOT: No, but I get you! I get you well!

MR. ELLIOT: What are you on about?

MRS. ELLIOT: You're going to sell the house and throw us into the street!

MR. ELLIOT: You mean into the avenue.

MRS. ELLIOT: Just try it! Just try it!

MR. ELLIOT: You don't really think that.

MRS. ELLIOT: You don't know what I think.

MR. ELLIOT: You just *want* to think it.

MRS. ELLIOT: You said you would.

MR. ELLIOT (*suddenly wearily*): I said I would what?

MRS. ELLIOT: You said you'd sell the house.

MR. ELLIOT: I . . . threatened . . . to sell the house.

MRS. ELLIOT: Huh! Threatened!

MR. ELLIOT: Yes . . . I *threatened* to sell the house. (*Pause.*) You forced me to.

MRS. ELLIOT: Don't blame me for what you've done.

MR. ELLIOT (*more excited*): *You* were threatening *me*!

MRS. ELLIOT (*sarcastic*): *Me* threatening *you*? Ahhhh . . . poor babby!

MR. ELLIOT: You said you were going to make me pay.

MRS. ELLIOT (*bitter*): Her pay.

MR. ELLIOT: What?

MRS. ELLIOT: I said I was going to make *her* pay.
    (*Silence.* MRS. ELLIOT *turns to look at him. Then intensely.*)
    Your slut.

MR. ELLIOT (*glances around*): I've only got *one* slut.

MRS. ELLIOT (*ignoring him*): I wonder how she'd like it? I wonder how she'd feel if I did go and see her family . . . and told them what she is? What she's *really* like? A dirty little slut

who hangs around the clubs . . . after the old men . . . the
married men . . . the worn-out whoremasters! Because she
can't get a man of her own! I wonder what her family would
say?

MR. ELLIOT: They'd say: 'Oh.'

MRS. ELLIOT: Eh?

MR. ELLIOT: OH!

MRS. ELLIOT (*raging*): YOU'LL SEE!

MR. ELLIOT (*goading*): Don't forget about the office . . .

MRS. ELLIOT: You're so cocky . . .

MR. ELLIOT: Weren't you going to phone her boss and give him
a character reference too?

MRS. ELLIOT: You'll see!

MR. ELLIOT: I'll see what?

MRS. ELLIOT: You'll see . . .

MR. ELLIOT: So will you . . .

(*Silence.* MR. ELLIOT *stares at her.*)

You know why I threatened to sell the house. I don't *wish* to
do so. I know the kids like it here . . . they've got plenty of
friends in the road . . . and the school's convenient . . . and
I know you like it . . . the neighbours . . .

MRS. ELLIOT (*sobs*): Pitied!

MR. ELLIOT (*stunned*): Eh?

MRS. ELLIOT: Pitied by all of them!

MR. ELLIOT: Eh? Pitied? BALLS! You like to imagine you're an
object of pity. It makes you feel noble. (*Mounting
frustration.*) You like to think you're the talk of the
wash-house . . . (*Old woman's voice.*) 'That poor, benighted
girl . . . so cruelly forsaken . . . a martyr to her husband's
lusts . . . bravely devoting her life to her two lovely little
children, struggling to give them a decent upbringing . . .
but oh! abandoned and alone . . . while her swine of a
husband squanders the family income on the services of
sluts and the company of drunkards!'

MRS. ELLIOT (*laughs*): That sounds a fair description.

MR. ELLIOT (*carried away; raging*): Hypocrites! I know how they
look at me when I come down the road. 'Look out,' they
whisper. 'Here comes Mr. Elliot, the black sheep of

Greengate Avenue. Bring in the children and bolt the doors!' And the truth of the matter is . . . is that half the men are practising quiet, civilized adultery and the other half are aching for it . . . but without any nasty messy wounding things like *relationships* . . . and half the women would be only too happy if the men had a quiet, civilized thrombosis tonight! As long as there was no social stigma and the insurance was up to date.

MRS. ELLIOT: Does that make you feel better?

(*Silence.* MRS. ELLIOT *turns to face him.*)

MR. ELLIOT (*jaunty*): Well . . . at least I'm honest about it!

MRS. ELLIOT: What do you want? A medal?

MR. ELLIOT: A word of recognition will do . . . or just a quiet ovation.

MRS. ELLIOT: You are a bastard!

MR. ELLIOT: I'm an honest bastard.

MRS. ELLIOT (*contemptuous*): Honest! You go on about honesty as if it meant a general amnesty. (*Pause. Then mocking.*) 'I destroyed my children, but I'm honest about it . . .' If every criminal was honest, it wouldn't reduce the crime rate!

(*Silence.*)

MR. ELLIOT (*measured*): I am not 'destroying the children'. I might have destroyed them had I stayed with you.

MRS. ELLIOT: Huh!

MR. ELLIOT: I'm not going to say that I left you purely 'for the sake of the children'.

MRS. ELLIOT: No . . . you're not!

MR. ELLIOT: . . . but they certainly suffer less from the separation than they did from the union!

MRS. ELLIOT: Because they see less of you . . .

MR. ELLIOT: Because they see less of . . . us. (*Opens door, listens, closes it.*) You miss that, don't you? (*Bitter.*) You enjoyed those . . . performances. (*Compère's voice.*) 'THE VIRTUOUS MRS. ELLIOT EXPOSES THE WICKED MR. ELLIOT TO THE INNOCENT LITTLE ELLIOTS.'

MRS. ELLIOT: *They had a right to know.*

MR. ELLIOT (*emphatic*): They had a right *not* to know! (*Pause;*

turning away.) Christ . . . we're off again. (*Recites.*) You say alpha, I say beta, you say gamma, I say delta . . . the dance of the dead language. (*Pause; now recovering.*) You know . . . I think that was the worst thing about those performances. We exposed the innocent little Elliots to such a storm of obsolete phrases. Oh, we went at it with a will . . . with whoops and war cries . . . a home-made Western, with rusty guns and rubber arrows. (*Pause; a bit sadly.*) It was poor stuff . . . (*More cheerfully.*) Well . . . at least . . . they'll pass any examination on the more obvious miseries of marriage, won't they?

(MRS. ELLIOT *has not been listening to this speech. Silence. Her foot jerks.* MR. ELLIOT *stares at her.*)

(*Pleading.*) I want the children to have a chance. And I want us to have a chance . . . you . . . me . . . but we have no chance, none of us, while you and I are together. We've tried it . . . it didn't work. All I'm trying to do . . . is to work out a way of life that I can live . . . live honestly . . . without going bent, or collecting little boys or something. Why won't *you* try? Why?

(MRS. ELLIOT *sits staring.* MR. ELLIOT *moves to the window, looks out at the garden. Turns and glances at the kitchen, then looks critically round the lounge.*)

(*Harsh.*) What are you trying to do? Hound me with guilt? (*Pause.*) Pressurize me back here? You won't!

(*He moves back and stands in front of* MRS. ELLIOT, *who ignores him.*)

I know your tactics. This act. This 'sloth pitch'. (*Pause; then venomous.*) You're *willing* the weeds to grow and the spiders to spin and the trays to rust . . . aren't you?

(*He puts his hands on the chair, leaning over* MRS. ELLIOT. *His voice is ugly with anger.*)

You can sit and stare till Doomsday but you won't STARE ME BACK!

(*Silence.*)

MRS. ELLIOT (*grimly*): Are you living with that slut?
MR. ELLIOT (*stunned*): Eh?
MRS. ELLIOT: You are . . . aren't you?

MR. ELLIOT (*evasive*): What?

MRS. ELLIOT (*snaps*): Has *she* got a washing machine . . .

MR. ELLIOT (*thrown*): Eh? *You've* got a washing machine . . .

MRS. ELLIOT: . . . that doesn't work!

MR. ELLIOT (*recovery—deadpan. Pause*): Actually we live in a penthouse with a colour television suspended from the ceiling and eat . . . only at the best restaurants. (*Pause; then aggressive.*) Why did you ring me?

MRS. ELLIOT: Huh.

MR. ELLIOT (*sits down*): I refuse to be trapped.

MRS. ELLIOT: You trapped yourself.

MR. ELLIOT: You set the trap.

MRS. ELLIOT: You trapped both of us!

MR. ELLIOT: And freed both of us.

MRS. ELLIOT: You're not FREE!

MR. ELLIOT: No? (*Pause; sings, romantic croon.*) 'I'll never be free-eeeee, from you and me-eeee . . .' (*Pause; then bitterly.*) Christ . . . I'm beginning to believe it too!

MRS. ELLIOT (*satisfied*): It's true.

MR. ELLIOT (*explodes*): BALLS!

(*Silence.* MR. ELLIOT *walks to the window* (*muttering* 'Alphabetagammadeltaalpha') *and back. Faces* MRS. ELLIOT.) (*Bitter but measured.*) *Why* are you so determined to get me back here? (*Pause.*) Why? (*Then with a touch of desperation.*) Are you still in love with me or what?

MRS. ELLIOT (*flinches*): Huh . . .

MR. ELLIOT (*insistent*): Or . . . do you just want your pound of flesh?

MRS. ELLIOT (*stubborn*): I want what I'm entitled to.

MR. ELLIOT: What's that?

(*Silence.* MRS. ELLIOT *stares ahead.* MR. ELLIOT *stands facing her.*)

And what's that?

MRS. ELLIOT: You know what that is . . .

MR. ELLIOT: I don't. I don't know.

MRS. ELLIOT: Oh . . . don't you?

MR. ELLIOT: No . . . I don't know.

(*Silence.*)

You mean you're entitled to keep me in misery for the rest of my life?

MRS. ELLIOT (*snaps*): YES!

MR. ELLIOT: You're doing it anyway. (*Pause.*) But you're not *entitled* to do it.

MRS. ELLIOT: I am.

MR. ELLIOT: You're not.

MRS. ELLIOT: I am.

MR. ELLIOT: You are not!

MRS. ELLIOT: I am!

MR. ELLIOT (*grim patience*): *How* are you entitled to do it?

MRS. ELLIOT: By the law.

MR. ELLIOT: What law?

MRS. ELLIOT: *The* law.

MR. ELLIOT: That is not the law.

MRS. ELLIOT: It *is* the law.
(*Pause.*)

MR. ELLIOT: That is *not* the law! (*Pause.*) What law is that? The law says that you can marry and you can separate and you can, in certain circumstances, dissolve the marriage. You are *not* entitled to hound me! (*Pause.*) What law?

MRS. ELLIOT (*shouts*): The MORAL law!

MR. ELLIOT (*stubborn*): What moral law?

MRS. ELLIOT: *The* moral law.

MR. ELLIOT: You won't make it any clearer by parrotting it out. The moral law . . . the moral law . . . what moral law?

MRS. ELLIOT (*very confident*): There's only one moral law.

MR. ELLIOT: You mean the law of the Jews two thousand years ago? (*Pause.*) They had their tablets—we have ours! (*Laughs.*) Every country has its own moral laws and they differ at different times. What would you be saying now if you lived in . . . (*Searching for a word.*) . . . Outer Polynesia? (*Pause—then heated.*) You know what I think is immoral? To perpetuate a destructive marriage. And it's especially immoral to do it 'for the sake of the children'. Because then you also perpetuate a destructive cycle that they will inherit.

MRS. ELLIOT: Why don't you go and live in Outer Polynesia?

MR. ELLIOT: I want the system changed!

MRS. ELLIOT: You want people changed.

MR. ELLIOT (*scornfully*): Go on . . . tell me . . . 'People are the same everywhere'. They certainly manage to conceal their similarities! Maybe all of us . . . maybe we all want to feed and sleep and shag and crap . . . but we certainly devise different ways of organizing the process. (*Pause; then bitterly.*) And here . . . here in this little corner of the human nest . . . we've devised our own brand of organizing the mating and breeding process . . . West European Monogamy, *perpetua dormienda*! But the trouble is, the women are breaking out of the nest. They want more. They don't want to be stuck in the nest forever.
(*Silence.*)
Christ . . . only in the last century men could *sell* their wives in the market place . . . and there are quite a few who'd do it today given the opportunity! But it's all changing . . . people are changing . . . and the system has got to change too.
(*Pause.*)
Because women are growing up. The old-fashioned Mammie—like you—won't put up with Big Daddy's casual shags down the Dock Road or after the office party . . . she won't turn a blind eye like Grannie did. She blows up and issues ultimatums. When she says 'You're mine', she really means it.
While the new-fashioned Mammie, with her job and her car and her see-through bra, she wants a bit of what's going, for herself. *Her* credo is: If you shag, I shag. So the poor old male gets hammered either way . . . and he just can't stand it.
And marriage . . . as we've known it . . . marriage can't stand it either. I don't know whether we're going to develop some concept of 'Serial Marriage', where everyone *expects* to have a series of partners . . . Hollywood-style. Or whether we're just going to develop a new-style relationship that's permanent as long as it lasts . . . but with a hell of a lot more honesty from the beginning.

But one thing is certain . . . in future, men and women
are going to share free and equal unions that last because
they want them to last. Not because they're forced! And
not because anybody *owns* anybody. Nobody *can* own
anybody! (*Pause; then almost fervently.*) Free men . . . will
live freely . . . with free women!

MRS. ELLIOT: And who's going to bring up the children?

MR. ELLIOT: Professionals.

MRS. ELLIOT: Professional what?

MR. ELLIOT: Pedagogues. People who freely choose to look after
children.

MRS. ELLIOT: You mean . . . you'd put the children in a home?

MR. ELLIOT (*explodes*): I'd put all the children of the world in a
home! To learn to love. And I'd put all the adults of the
world *in the world*. To learn to live. (*Pause.*) Oh, I know
there'd always be a few frightened savages who'd prefer to
stay down in the family pits . . . but the majority would
jump at the chance of freedom.

(*Pause.* MRS. ELLIOT *stares at the window.* MR. ELLIOT *stares
at her.*)

(*Intones like a butler.*) You rang?

(*Silence.*)

Why did you ring me up?

MRS. ELLIOT: Did we disturb you?

MR. ELLIOT: What was the matter?

MRS. ELLIOT (*mimicking*): What was the matter?

MR. ELLIOT: I dashed up here.

MRS. ELLIOT: Ahhh . . . did you?

(*Silence.*)

I was going to kill myself . . . and the children.

(*Silence.*)

MR. ELLIOT: Were you?

MRS. ELLIOT: So I poured three glasses of Nembutal . . . to 'end
it all'.

MR. ELLIOT: You should have poured one for me too.

MRS. ELLIOT: You're welcome . . .

MR. ELLIOT: And why did you ring me? Did you want me to
stop you . . . or just to watch?

MRS. ELLIOT: I just thought you'd like to know.

(MR. ELLIOT *goes to the table and examines the glasses.*)

MR. ELLIOT: Is this it?

MRS. ELLIOT: Drink and see.

MR. ELLIOT: Well, as I always say . . . suicide's the one thing you never regret. (*Pause.*) You haven't had any of this already, by any chance?

MRS. ELLIOT: Huh.

MR. ELLIOT: You haven't, have you? (*Pause.*) And the kids . . . they're all right, aren't they?

MRS. ELLIOT: You saw them.

MR. ELLIOT: Are they?

MRS. ELLIOT: Yes.

MR. ELLIOT: I can't have you despatching *all* my problems at once, you know.

(*Long pause.* MRS. ELLIOT *sits still.* MR. ELLIOT *looks at her, then goes to the window and looks out. It is getting darker now. After a while he goes into the garden and collects the bicycle. He comes back in with it.*)

Have you got a rag?

(MRS. ELLIOT *fetches a rag from the kitchen.*)

Don't want this going rusty.

(*He dries off the bicycle.*)

These brakes need tightening up . . . (*He works on the brakes.*) What did this cost? About thirty quid . . . wasn't it? (*Chuckles.*) Christ . . . I remember my first bike. A sit up and beg. My mam got it from a dump in Scotland Road . . . for fifteen bob . . . a real old wreck, but it went. (*Pause.*) Actually that old bike went for four years . . . then I sold it for nine bob. (*Pause; works on brakes, tests them.*) Then the old man took me into town for my fifteenth birthday and bought me a new Raleigh Sports . . . on the never-never, of course . . . I think that was the first H.P. form he signed in his life and he never really recovered. (*Laughs.*) It had low-slung handlebars . . . real racy . . . I painted it red and white. I had that bike for years and years . . . went everywhere on it.

MRS. ELLIOT: You left it at the flat.

MR. ELLIOT: Eh?

MRS. ELLIOT: Don't you remember? You left it at the first flat we had. You were always going to go back and get it, but . . . don't you remember?

MR. ELLIOT: Oh . . . yes . . . well, no, actually. I've got a lousy memory . . . it's self-deleting. (*Pause.*) My greatest gift! (*Silence.*)

MRS. ELLIOT: I walked past that place last week.

MR. ELLIOT: Which?

MRS. ELLIOT: The house . . . they had a new fence round the garden . . . about six feet high . . . you couldn't see in.

MR. ELLIOT: Oh . . .

MRS. ELLIOT: Remember the old fence and the time it crashed into the street?

(*Pause.* MR. ELLIOT *busies himself with the bike.*)

You had to take a day off work trying to get it back up.

MR. ELLIOT (*uncomfortable*): Yeah . . . (*Pause.*) Does Tony let Sarah ride this?

MRS. ELLIOT: He would . . . but I won't.

MR. ELLIOT: It's big for her, yet.

MRS. ELLIOT: She tries to ride it in the garden. (*Smiles.*) If she had her way she'd be off down the motorway with it!

MR. ELLIOT: Huh!

MRS. ELLIOT: She's headstrong. (*Pause.*) She's got your . . . confidence.

MR. ELLIOT: You know what she said to me on Sunday? She said: 'I *might* get married when I grow up . . . but I'm not going to marry a drunkard like you.'

MRS. ELLIOT: Hmmm.

MR. ELLIOT (*now nervously fiddling with the bike*): This needs a drop of oil.

(MRS. ELLIOT *fetches oil from the kitchen and watches him.*)

MRS. ELLIOT: Sarah's a bit deceptive, though. She's got bags of confidence outwardly . . . in company . . . but underneath she's nervous . . . very impressionable. (*Pause.*) Tony's just the opposite. He won't open his mouth in company—he's a real gooseberry! People pat him on the head and tell him not to be shy and you can see him wilting on the spot. But all the time . . . underneath . . . he's really very sure of himself. In fact . . . he's probably *too* sure. He's arrogant.

(MR. ELLIOT *finishes with the bike and puts it in the hallway.*)

MR. ELLIOT: That should be O.K.

(MR. ELLIOT *comes back in and stands uncertainly. He goes to the sideboard and picks up a letter.*)

MRS. ELLIOT: I think it's the gas bill.

MR. ELLIOT (*opening it*): Four pounds eighteen . . . that's not bad.

MRS. ELLIOT: We haven't used much . . . with the warm weather.

MR. ELLIOT: Did the man come about the telly?

MRS. ELLIOT: No . . . I waited in, but there was no sign of him.

MR. ELLIOT: Can you get a picture?

MRS. ELLIOT: Just about.

MR. ELLIOT: I'll give him a tinkle tomorrow.

MRS. ELLIOT: I'm not bothered really . . . but the children like to watch.

MR. ELLIOT: Yeah . . . I'll ring him tomorrow. What day?

MRS. ELLIOT: What?

MR. ELLIOT: What day shall I ask him to come?

MRS. ELLIOT: Any day. I'm in every day.

MR. ELLIOT (*uncomfortable*): Yeah . . . well, I'll ask him to come as soon as possible.

(*Silence.*)

MRS. ELLIOT: Did you see the photograph?

MR. ELLIOT (*looking*): Oh . . . when was that taken?

MRS. ELLIOT: Last week . . . at school.

MR. ELLIOT: Look at Sarah saying 'Cheese'. (*Laughs.*) Tony looks distinctly mutinous.

MRS. ELLIOT: He hates having his photograph taken.

(MRS. ELLIOT *gets up.*)

I'll make a cup of coffee.

MR. ELLIOT: Oh . . . thanks.

MRS. ELLIOT (*going*): There's a couple of snapshots there too.

MR. ELLIOT (*looking at them*): They're not bad, are they?

MRS. ELLIOT (*from kitchen*): They were only a shilling each.

(*Pause.* MR. ELLIOT *stares at the three glasses.*)

MR. ELLIOT: What about the big one?

MRS. ELLIOT: That was twelve and six.

MR. ELLIOT: I'll give you the money.

MRS. ELLIOT: Oh . . . thanks.

> (MR. ELLIOT *looks at the photographs as* MRS. ELLIOT *comes in with the coffee, puts it on the floor, and sits on the couch.* MR. ELLIOT *glances slightly nervously at her as she sits, then looks back at the snapshots.* MRS. ELLIOT *sits back, much more relaxed now.*)

MR. ELLIOT (*almost shy*): Can I have one?

MRS. ELLIOT: One is for you.

MR. ELLIOT (*awkwardly*): Oh . . . right. (*Pause.*) Thanks. (*Pause.*) They look great. (*Long pause.*) I feel very proud of them.

MRS. ELLIOT: Hm.

> (*Silence.* MR. ELLIOT *sighs heavily.*)

Still sighing?

MR. ELLIOT: Eh?

MRS. ELLIOT: You never stop sighing these days.

MR. ELLIOT: It's a plea for sympathy . . .

MRS. ELLIOT: Huh . . .

> (*Silence.* MR. ELLIOT *stares absently.* MRS. ELLIOT *looks at him from the side.*)

You're beginning to spread . . .

MR. ELLIOT: I drink too much.

MRS. ELLIOT: So what's new?

MR. ELLIOT (*glum*): Now I drink too much too much.

MRS. ELLIOT (*sympathetic*): It's the Irish in you.

MR. ELLIOT: No . . . as the old man used to say . . . it's just genuine undiluted greed.

> (*Silence.*)

MRS. ELLIOT: Why don't you go and see him?

MR. ELLIOT (*flat*): I couldn't face him.

MRS. ELLIOT (*almost teasing*): That's not like you!

MR. ELLIOT: I don't want to hurt him . . .

MRS. ELLIOT: It's amazing how you can care so much about 'not hurting' people . . . yet you strew your casualties all over the place!

MR. ELLIOT: What casualties?

MRS. ELLIOT: Your father, now. Your mother . . . once. Your

children. Your . . . women. (*Pause.*) I know I'm not the
first to suffer . . . and I won't be the last. (*Pause.*) It's not
much of a consolation, but it's a help.
(*Silence.*)

MR. ELLIOT (*meaning it*): I *do* hate to hurt people.

MRS. ELLIOT: I know. I know you do. But you can't keep your
hands off people. You want to *save* them . . .

MR. ELLIOT: Save them?

MRS. ELLIOT: You're a real old Catholic missionary at heart.
(*Laughs.*) Maybe you should have gone to Outer Polynesia!
You're drawn to people . . . like me, once . . . who are
lonely, or shy, or . . . in some way, incomplete . . . and you
can't rest until you . . . *complete* them. You offer them *your*
vitality, *your* resilience, *your* confidence . . . but instead of
saving anybody, you're actually enslaving them. (*Pause.*)
It's funny to hear you going on about not 'owning' people,
because in fact you insist on owning any woman you're in
love with . . . that's your price . . . you have to *own*
her—heart and mind and body, and past and present and
future too! You . . . infiltrate . . . every particle. (*Pause.*) I
feel sorry for you because I think you're innocent. (*Pause.*)
But that's why you're so dangerous . . . because when
you've satisfied your missionary zeal . . . when you've got
your new convert, now dedicated, completely committed to
you . . . what happens then? (*Pause.*) You drop her!
BUMP! Down to earth again. And off you go galloping on
your next crusade! (*Pause. MR. ELLIOT turns to her.*)

MR. ELLIOT: All this . . . because I walked out on you?

MRS. ELLIOT: It's not just me.

MR. ELLIOT: You're the one who matters . . . to you.

MRS. ELLIOT: What about the first one?

MR. ELLIOT (*slightly edgy*): What first what?

MRS. ELLIOT (*now also edgy*): *Your* first one. (*Pause.*) The one that
you used to go on about.

MR. ELLIOT (*laughs*): My *first* permanent relationship? *She*
dropped me.

MRS. ELLIOT: Huh! After you drove her to it!
(*Silence. MRS. ELLIOT stares intensely at him from the side.*)

You know damn well that you would have dropped her if
she hadn't dropped you! But that . . . that was just what
you wanted her to do. You wanted the feeling of being
betrayed, abandoned, etc., etc., etc. . . . all the things you
accused me of enjoying . . . because you revelled in the
drama!
(*Silence.*)
What happened afterwards? When she came back . . .
wanting to talk to you? She was desperate . . . but did you
help her? (*Laughs.*) HUH! You wouldn't even talk to her.
You hid in the lavatory! A grown man hiding in the
lavatory from a girl who wants to talk! What a hero!
(MR. ELLIOT *flinches. Stares straight ahead.* MRS. ELLIOT
laughs sourly.)
But I wasn't so obliging, was I? I wouldn't leave you. You
had to leave me. *You* had to be the . . . 'betrayer'. And you
don't like that role nearly as much, do you? Your old
Catholic conscience gives you hell, doesn't it? (*Pause; then
acidly.*) That's if you still feel *anything*.

MR. ELLIOT: As you ask . . .

MRS. ELLIOT: I didn't!

MR. ELLIOT: . . . As you evidently feel some curiosity about my
spiritual condition, it might help you to know that I have
enough anguish, guilt and remorse swilling about inside me
to float a bloody monastery!

MRS. ELLIOT: You should have gone on the stage.

MR. ELLIOT (*ignores her*): And if, to that brew, I add about ten
pints of bitter ale, I can just about lurch from one derelict
sunset to another. (*Laughs—bravado tone.*) I'm an apostolic
alcoholic!
(*Long pause.* MR. ELLIOT *is slumped back in the chair. The sun
is now low in the sky.* MRS. ELLIOT *glances at him. He rouses
himself suddenly. His tone is weary and self-disgusted.*)
Christ . . . I'm tired of them!

MRS. ELLIOT (*cautious*): What?

MR. ELLIOT: All my . . . untethered agonies. (*Pause; then in a
firm, common-sense tone.*) Can't we be practical?
(MRS. ELLIOT *does not reply or look at him.*)

We've been separated for three years. The law—the *law*—allows us to divorce by mutual consent after two years. (*Then nervously.*) We could do that now. (*Silence.*) But it also allows unilateral divorce after *five* years. So that I can divorce you, without your consent, in two years from now. (*Pause.*) Which I *will*. (*Pause.*) Why the hell not face up to it now, start again, get a job . . . (*Then pleading.*) You know I'll look after you and the kids . . . (*Now forceful.*) So why not be adult about the situation and——

MRS. ELLIOT (*snaps*): What about her?

MR. ELLIOT: Who?

MRS. ELLIOT: YOUR SLUT!

(*Pause.* MR. ELLIOT *looks grim but ignores her.*)

How long is that going to last?

MR. ELLIOT: It's a permanent relationship.

MRS. ELLIOT: Huh! The only permanent relationships you have are with the past!

MR. ELLIOT: She's my last and only love.

MRS. ELLIOT: Huh . . .

MR. ELLIOT: You think I'm beyond redemption?

MRS. ELLIOT: Beyond repair.

(*Pause. Then with some exasperation.*)

MR. ELLIOT: Look . . . what are *you* suggesting we do? Are you suggesting we play the social game? So I live here . . . on a loose rein . . . and I'm allowed out every Friday night for some wild revel in the woods, after which I return— exhausted and seed-freed—to the old barred cell? Balls! I'm through with all that.

(*Pause.* MR. ELLIOT *walks to the window. Very restless. His tone is urgent now, sincere.*)

Look . . . there's no need for . . . despair! O.K., you *may* wonder about the neighbours . . . but it's a nine-day wonder with them and they're probably consumed with envy in any case. (*Pause.*) They don't matter. (*Pause.*) And the children . . . I have a better relationship with them than I ever had. I used to curse their existence but now I . . . I'm proud of them, I'm happy with them . . . I love them, for Christ's sake!

MRS. ELLIOT (*harsh*): Because they're older . . .

MR. ELLIOT (*snaps*): Not just because they're *older* . . .
    because . . .
    (*Pause.*)

MRS. ELLIOT: What?

MR. ELLIOT (*determined*): I'm happier with them because I'm
    happier without them.

MRS. ELLIOT: Hmmm.
    (*Pause.* MR. ELLIOT *turns to face her. She moves to the chair
    facing the window.*)

MR. ELLIOT: I wish it was simpler. . . . You're an attractive
    woman . . . a good, selfless mother . . . and a jealous,
    vindictive wife. I wish you were just a one-hundred-per-
    cent bitch. It'd be a hell of a lot easier!

MRS. ELLIOT (*sarcastic*): I'm sorry . . .

MR. ELLIOT (*very serious*): Can I tell you something you won't
    believe?
    (*Silence.*)
    I have no wish to hurt you.
    (*She looks at him sourly.*)
    I don't want to damage you! I know your quality . . . and I
    don't want to humiliate you, to cheat you, to exploit you
    . . . to emotionally destroy you. That's why I left you!
    (*Silence.*)

MRS. ELLIOT (*withering*): Thanks.

MR. ELLIOT (*dispirited*): Ahhh.

MRS. ELLIOT (*cynical*): Still the old saviour? (*Laughs.*) Listen, the
    truth is, you do exactly what you want to do and you don't
    give a bugger who you destroy in the process. So . . . so
    carry on, do what you want to do, but just don't ask for my
    blessing.

MR. ELLIOT: And what about you? Aren't you trying to force me
    to do what *you* want me to do?

MRS. ELLIOT: Only the things you undertook—vowed—to do!

MR. ELLIOT: Oh—not again!

MRS. ELLIOT: So you did.

MR. ELLIOT: So I did . . . subject to satisfaction.

MRS. ELLIOT: You can't have marriage on free approval.

MR. ELLIOT (*heated*): And when a marriage breaks down—there's no law that would tolerate this sort of emotional blackmail! (*Points to the glasses.*) This . . . there's no law, moral or otherwise, that entitles you to threaten that you will kill yourself and murder the children . . . just so that you can 'have your way' with your errant husband.

MRS. ELLIOT: My knight-errant husband.

MR. ELLIOT (*raging*): It's just blackmail!

MRS. ELLIOT (*deadly pleasant*): You know . . . you've given me an idea. If you really want to help . . . (*Pause.* MR. ELLIOT *looks at her.*) It would be easier . . . and tidier . . . and we know how you care about tidiness . . . if *you* took the deadly draught, wouldn't it? Not here, of course . . . not in this room . . . (*Light laugh.*) You wouldn't want any corpses littering the lounge and frightening the children, would you? But somewhere . . . I know! In your penthouse! What about that? In your penthouse! Suicide seems more appropriate to a penthouse anyway, doesn't it? (*Very brightly.*) And I tell you what . . . maybe *she* would take a sip too . . . from the same glass! Yes . . . maybe you could *share the same glass* of nembutal, with different straws, of course . . . and sink simultaneously down together . . . like you always wanted! Then the children and I . . . would live happily ever after. How about that?

(*Silence.* MR. ELLIOT *gives several slow handclaps.*)

MR. ELLIOT (*urbane, philosophic tone*): Yes, it's true. . . . Marriage is one of the few surviving forms of ritual slaughter.

MRS. ELLIOT: Oh well . . . (*Brightly.*) You're going to change everything, aren't you? You're going to change the system?

MR. ELLIOT (*amused*): Yes . . . I think I shall switch my efforts to saving society.

MRS. ELLIOT: You're going to shatter the system . . .

MR. ELLIOT (*smug*): *Yes.*

MRS. ELLIOT: . . . which still satisfies the vast majority

MR. ELLIOT: I'm a social catalyst.

MRS. ELLIOT (*withering*): A social misfit.

MR. ELLIOT: Omega.

MRS. ELLIOT: What?

MR. ELLIOT: The language of love.

MRS. ELLIOT: *You're* the linguist!

MR. ELLIOT (*childlike recitation*):

> 'Love that's loved from day to day
> Loves itself into decay . . .'

MRS. ELLIOT: Remember that . . . for future reference.
(*Pause.*)

MR. ELLIOT: No . . . we should never have married.

MRS. ELLIOT (*brittle*): *We* should never have met.

MR. ELLIOT (*theatrical*): WE should never have been born!

MRS. ELLIOT (*vicious*): Somebody should have *told* your mother.
(MR. ELLIOT *goes to slap her, but stops.*)

MR. ELLIOT: You slut . . .

MRS. ELLIOT: You buck . . .

MR. ELLIOT: I'm going.
(MR. ELLIOT *moves to go . . . looks at the glasses . . .
hesitates.*)

MRS. ELLIOT: Go on then . . . (*Shouts.*) GO!
(MR. ELLIOT *puts on his coat.*)

MR. ELLIOT: Are you going to be sensible?

MRS. ELLIOT (*harsh*): Are you going to grow up?

MR. ELLIOT (*a plea*): You'll have to come to terms with it.

MRS. ELLIOT: I have done.

MR. ELLIOT (*surprised*): What?

MRS. ELLIOT (*confident*): My terms.

MR. ELLIOT: What do you mean?

MRS. ELLIOT: I've come to *my* terms.

MR. ELLIOT: I don't accept *your* terms.

MRS. ELLIOT: You will.
(*Silence.* MR. ELLIOT *turns decisively and moves to the door.*)

MR. ELLIOT: I'll see you on Sunday . . . usual time.

MRS. ELLIOT: If you go through that door . . . I'll kill myself
and the children.
(*Silence.* MR. ELLIOT *turns at the door and stares at her.
Long pause. He tugs at his coat.*)

MR. ELLIOT: I'll see you on Sunday . . . at 2.15 . . . as usual.
(*He goes.*)

(MRS. ELLIOT *stares after him. Then she gets up, goes to the glasses. She looks at them. She takes hold of one. Pause. She takes all three in her hands and takes them to the kitchen. She hurls them into the sink.*)
(*She returns, stops, looks at door, listens. Pause. Then she sits. Her foot jerks. She ignores it and remains staring straight ahead.*)

CURTAIN